Sustaining Thought

Thirty Years of Cookery at SAR

LESLIE SHIPMAN

with ROSEMARY CARSTENS

SCHOOL FOR ADVANCED RESEARCH ON THE HUMAN EXPERIENCE

School for Advanced Research Press
Post Office Box 2188
Santa Fe, New Mexico 87504-2188
www.sarpress.sarweb.org

Co-Director and Executive Editor: Catherine Cocks
Copy Editor: Rosemary Carstens
Designer and Production Manager: Cynthia Dyer
Proofreaders: James Douglas, Catherine Cocks, Kate Whelan
Indexers: James Douglas, Catherine Cocks
Printer: Edwards Brothers, Inc.

Library of Congress Cataloging-in-Publication Data:
Shipman, Leslie.
Sustaining thought : thirty years of cookery at the School for Advanced Research /
Leslie Shipman, with Rosemary Carstens.
p. cm.
Includes index.
ISBN 1-930618-83-2 (pa : alk. paper)
1. Cookery. 2. Menus. 3. School for Advanced Research (Santa Fe, N.M.)
I Carstens, Rosemary. II. School for Advanced Research (Santa Fe, N.M.). III Title.

TX714.S5426 2007
641.—dc22
2006029735

Cover illustration: SAR Seminar House dining room © 2006 School for Advanced Research.
Illustration by Cynthia Dyer from a photograph by Jason S. Ordaz.
All other illustrations © School for Advanced Research, by Cynthia Dyer
from photographs by Katrina Lasko, Jonathan Lewis, and Jason S. Ordaz.

Table of Contents

SAR and the Art of Dining

Sustaining Thought is what the School for Advanced Research (SAR) is all about. Since its founding in 1907 as a center for the study of the ancient Americas, the School has expanded its mission to encompass the world and helped thousands of scholars explore the mysteries of human culture and evolution. Fine cooking is one of life's most pleasurable experiences and sharing meals one of the key means of building human community, so we take both seriously. When researchers gather here to add to the sum of human knowledge through a seminar in Santa Fe, our delicious, home-cooked meals nourish and delight the body just as the conversations nourish and delight the mind.

Over dinner, our guests forge new friendships and discover new opportunities to teach and to learn. "Those relationships continued to grow and flourish long after the seminar and [the] book were over," reflected one visiting scholar. "It was a marvelous way for younger scholars to get noticed and for established scholars to become interested in your work. They would be very generous afterwards." One group met to critique the very idea of "community," so often used with careless abandon in public discussions. "Our efforts ended up constituting a community of participants," the chairman wrote ruefully, and he blamed the School for being too good a host.

What has worked so well for us we now offer to you in this cookbook. Unfolding around the seasons of our academic year, it contains recipes for breakfasts, lunches, and dinners tested by generations of our guests and fine-tuned by distinguished cooks and chefs. The recipes are perfect for that medium-size gathering and designed to take advantage of the best fresh foods of each season. Our seminars last about six days, so each chapter offers you six dinners, five lunches, and six breakfasts. If you're looking for complete menus, they're here, or you can mix and match to suit your tastes.

In our early days, Nita Schwartz, the wife of the School's then-president Douglas W. Schwartz, entertained and fed our visiting scholars. For a crew of archaeologists working on the North Rim of the Grand Canyon, she even "made some pretty good skillet biscuits" on a Coleman stove. As our programs grew, so too did our need for a permanent cook and kitchen crew. Sarah Wimett oversaw the SAR kitchen for many years while simultaneously running well-known restaurants in Santa Fe, including O. J. Sarah's on Guadalupe Street. Today, Leslie Shipman reigns over the historic ten-bedroom adobe home where our visitors debate big questions and eat with great relish. From mouthwatering entrees to mid-afternoon snacks calculated to calm high tempers or stimulate sleepy minds, Leslie makes the SAR experience a satisfying and memorable one for scores of visitors every year. These recipes give you the chance to make your guests leave beaming and beg to return, as do so many of our alumni!

From the Seminar House Kitchen

I am not a chef. I have never taken a cooking class, but I love to cook and to share the results with those around me. It probably has something to do with coming from a large family, marrying into an even larger family, and being surrounded by many, many fine cooks. I learned to bake chocolate chip cookies with my sister; to make doughnuts and fresh blueberry pies on a wood-burning stove in northern Minnesota with one grandmother; to snap and string beans on my Albuquerque grandmother's back porch; and I watched my mother cook for a houseful and never lose her graciousness. All of those wonderful and simple experiences gave me my introduction to cooking. As I grew older, I began to experiment, in secret, in my own kitchen. My family and friends rarely balked at what I placed in front of them. They didn't always clean their plates, either, but no one ever got sick and they faithfully followed up with thank-you notes full of suggestions on how to improve (or eliminate) the meals they shared in my home.

When I got married, my mother-in-law Frances brought a whole new dimension of culinary experiences into my life. She was in her late seventies by the time I met her, had raised six children, incorporated green chile into many of her family's southern recipes, and hosted hundreds of large, international dinner parties and political barbeques at her Pojoaque Jail House Ranch. Frances was a grand entertainer, and many of the recipes I use today originated in her kitchen.

As my children entered school, I was lucky to meet four of the finest kitchen wizards in Santa Fe: Jane, baker extraordinaire, author of several cookbooks, and the cofounder of the Santa Fe Public Schools program, "Cooking with Kids"; Southern California Katie, who raises chickens and fresh herbs in her backyard and does everything with a colorful, fresh, and experimental flare; Mary, who loves everything Italian and can create a cozy yet sophisticated evening in mere seconds; and my dear Casey, the neighbor with a great garden and a tremendous love of old friends, good food, and special wine, who will listen to my food musings and questions anytime I ask.

In the summer of 2000 I fell into the Seminar House slot with informal cooking experience and a large, loving support network. The enthusiasm and appreciation I receive from the School for Advanced Research staff and our many Seminar House guests encourage me to continue doing what I love. Thanks to them and to my wonderful family, my experiments continue. Every person has been a trusting, discriminating, and cooperative taste tester, even if he or she hadn't a clue at the time.

—L. S.

Altitude and Gratitude

Think of it this way: every time you begin to cook, you are launching a grand and delicious experiment. The recipes in this book result from many such experiments. Few are difficult, and all are sturdy enough to resist the effects of altitude high or low. But you should know that up in the rarefied mountain air of Santa Fe, water boils at a lower temperature and is cooler when it gets there. This means that it takes longer for liquids to come to a boil and then longer for them to cook the food in them. Also, breads and cakes rise more quickly. Readers living at lower altitudes should be conservative about baking times and keep an eye on the oven.

Here are some general tips: If you live between sea level and about 3,000 feet, you should shorten cooking times by five to ten minutes, lower baking temperatures by about 25° Fahrenheit, and, for baked goods, add slightly more leavening and slightly less liquid. Decrease flour by 1 tablespoon for every 1,500 feet lower in altitude. Increase liquids by about 1 to 2 tablespoons per cup for each 2,000 feet below 7,000 feet elevation.

Finally, a note about the origin of the many dog-eared and scribbled-on recipes in my files: like most cooks, I adapt and revise and taste-test dishes recommended by friends, clipped from magazines, and borrowed from cookbooks. Wherever possible, I give due credit to the source, but sometimes I've changed a recipe so much or had it for so long that even SAR's distinguished seminar participants wouldn't be able to figure out where it came from. If you recognize some old favorites here, please accept my compliments for sharing such a tasty recipe—and keep experimenting!

—L. S.

Autumn

Delicious autumn!
My very soul is wedded to it,
and if I were a bird
I would fly about the earth
seeking the successive autumns.
— *George Eliot*

There is a languor, a sultry savoring of each day that descends on Santa Fe in autumn. The scenery takes on drama, with sunny crisp days under clear, sharp blue skies and colder nights heralded by heavenly sunsets. By day there is the scent of roasting chiles, and in the evenings welcoming wafts of piñon burning in fireplaces. There are the fall and winter seasons of the Orchestra of Santa Fe, the Santa Fe Symphony, and Las Fiestas de Santa Fe (with its entire week of celebrations) to anticipate. It's a time for long, sauntering walks around town and meandering drives into the Sangre de Cristo Mountains.

About the middle of October, a band of gold appears at elevations above 8,000 feet as aspen groves show off their glory amidst splotches of dark green. Flocks of finches gather in large numbers, and it is not unusual to see Cassin's, rosy finches, pine siskins, and grosbeaks at Bandelier National Monument. In November, snow geese begin arriving at their winter feeding grounds and can be spotted especially at dawn and dusk as they vee their way across the sky.

At the School for Advanced Research, we welcome a new batch of scholars for one of our advanced seminars. These "seminarians," as we call them, hop out of the airport van in the School's parking lot on Saturday, excited and ready to be invigorated by their surroundings and the interaction with their fellow researchers.

WELCOME DINNER
Saturday

Beef Stew

Green Salad with Orange Vinaigrette

Rustic Farm Bread with Unsalted Butter

Apple Maple Cake

Beef Stew – serves 6

2 garlic cloves

⅓ cup vegetable oil

2 pounds lean beef (sirloin, chuck, or round), cut into 2-inch cubes

½ pound lean lamb, cut into 2-inch cubes

½ pound veal, cut into 2-inch cubes

2 large onions, sliced

¼ teaspoon thyme

½ teaspoon oregano

1 tablespoon salt

¼ cup coarsely chopped parsley

1 tablespoon unsalted butter

1¾ cups dry red wine

1½ cups water (enough to cover meat)

1½ pounds shelled peas and a handful of pods

4 tomatoes, quartered

8–10 pearl onions, peeled

6–8 carrots, sliced

¾ pound small mushrooms

1 teaspoon freshly ground black pepper

¾ cup wild rice

Rub a large stew pot with garlic cloves, discarding cloves after use. Heat oil and sear meat on all sides (you may have to do this in batches). Put all meat back into pot, add onions, and simmer until soft. Add thyme, oregano, salt, parsley, butter, ¾ cup red wine, and water. Cover and simmer 1½ hours. Add peas, pods, tomatoes, pearl onions, carrots, mushrooms, the remaining cup of red wine, and pepper. Mix ingredients together. Simmer 15 minutes. Stir in wild rice, cover, and simmer 1 hour. Uncover and simmer 15 minutes.

Ladle into bowls and garnish with parsley sprigs. Slices of fresh, warm rustic farm bread or other substantial white bread with unsalted butter are the perfect companion for this stew.

Apple Maple Cake – serves 8

2 cups all-purpose flour, sifted

2 teaspoons baking powder

½–¾ teaspoon ground ginger

1 teaspoon salt

4 tablespoons unsalted butter, softened

1¼ cups maple syrup

3 eggs

½ cup milk

1 Granny Smith apple, peeled and grated

½ cup chopped walnuts

Preheat oven to 350°F. Combine flour, baking powder, ginger, and salt in a bowl. Set aside. In a medium bowl, cream the butter with a mixer until smooth. Add the maple syrup in a slow stream and continue beating about 2 minutes. Add the eggs, one at a time, and increase mixer speed to medium-high. Beat until smooth and fluffy, about 5 minutes. Reduce speed to low and gradually beat in the flour mixture, then the milk, until smooth. Stir in the grated apple and walnuts, and then pour into a greased 10" cake pan. Bake until lightly golden and until a skewer inserted in the center comes out clean, 40–45 minutes. Cool 10 minutes before removing from the pan.

Top with ice cream or dollops of whipped cream lightly flavored with cinnamon.

Orange Vinaigrette*
makes 1 cup

¼ cup fresh orange or blood-orange juice

2 tablespoons minced shallots

1 tablespoon fresh thyme leaves

3 teaspoons grated orange peel

1 teaspoon honey

½ cup extra-virgin olive oil

¼ cup finely chopped fennel bulb

Mix first five ingredients together in small bowl. Slowly whisk olive oil into mixture until well blended. Add fennel bulb and stir gently.

Serve over a bed of fresh greens.

*May be refrigerated, covered, for up to 5 days.

Sunday – Day One
Breakfast

Buttermilk Waffles

Maple Syrup with Pine Nuts

Bacon

Melon Slices

Buttermilk Waffles – serves 5*

1 cup flour
2 teaspoons baking powder
¼ teaspoon salt
¼ cup vegetable oil
1 egg
buttermilk

Mix flour, baking powder, and salt in large bowl. Add vegetable oil and egg. Slowly mix in buttermilk, stirring constantly, until batter reaches the desired consistency. Heat waffle iron. Pour in one ladle of batter and cook until done.

*May be kept in 200°F oven, on oven racks (not on cookie sheets!), until ready to serve.

Maple Syrup with Pine Nuts – makes 2 cups

½ teaspoon salted butter
¼ cup pine nuts, coarsely chopped
2 cups real maple syrup

Melt butter in small frying pan. Add nuts and sauté on medium heat until nuts begin to brown. Pour the syrup into microwave-able container and add nuts. Using 30-second increments, slowly heat syrup mixture until desired temperature is reached. Do not boil! Serve in warmed pitcher.

Serve the waffles with crispy bacon slices, and finish off the meal with fresh melon.

Lunch

Smoked Mozzarella Sandwiches with Chile-Lime Mayonnaise
Baby Spinach Greens, Grated Carrot,
and Sliced Red Onion Salad with Balsamic Vinaigrette
Fruit Sorbet

Smoked Mozzarella Sandwiches – makes 10

20 slices good sourdough bread

20 sandwich slices smoked mozzarella cheese

4 6-ounce packages fresh basil leaves

2 10-ounce containers roasted red peppers, coarsely chopped

4 Granny Smith apples, peeled, cut in half, and thinly sliced

Lay 2 slices of bread out on counter top; generously spread chile-lime mayonnaise on both slices. Layer two pieces of cheese on one piece of bread. Place several basil leaves on top of cheese. Add 2 tablespoons of chopped red peppers and top with enough apple slices to cover. Top sandwich with second piece of bread. Cut in half on the diagonal, place on plate and cover with saran wrap until ready to serve. Continue constructing sandwiches until bread slices are gone.

Baby Spinach Greens, Grated Carrot, and Sliced Red Onion Salad with Balsamic Vinaigrette – serves 10

2 small packages baby spinach leaves

3 large carrots, peeled, cut in half, and finely grated

1 large red onion, peeled, halved, and cut into thin slices

Wash and stem spinach leaves. Place a handful on each plate. Sprinkle with several tablespoons of grated carrot and top with several crescents of red onion. Sprinkle with Balsamic Vinaigrette.

A light fruit sorbet makes a nice conclusion to this meal.

Chile-Lime Mayonnaise
make the night before

2 cups of your favorite mayonnaise

juice of 2 limes

3 teaspoons red chile powder

Mix all three ingredients together and refrigerate overnight to maximize flavor.

Balsamic Vinaigrette
makes 2 cups

½ cup balsamic vinegar

1 teaspoon sea salt

1½ cups extra-virgin olive oil

freshly ground black pepper to taste

Whisk the vinegar and salt together until the salt dissolves. Slowly whisk in the oil until the dressing is well blended.

Dinner

Broiled Lemon-Pepper Chicken Quarters

Orange Sweet Potatoes

Garlic-Roasted Green Beans with Shallots and Hazelnuts

Chocolate Spice Cake with Chocolate Fudge Frosting

Broiled Lemon-Pepper Chicken Quarters – serves 10

10 chicken quarters (leg and thigh)

extra-virgin olive oil

lemon-pepper seasoning

Position oven rack in upper third of oven, and turn on broiler. Rinse chicken quarters with cool water and pat dry. Place chicken quarters on broiling pan, skin side down, and drizzle with olive oil. Generously season with lemon-pepper seasoning and broil for 20 minutes or until they turn golden brown. Reduce temperature in oven to 300°F and bake for 15 minutes. Remove pan from oven and turn chicken over. Pour olive oil over chicken skin and generously sprinkle with lemon-pepper seasoning. Return to oven and cook at 300°F for 15 minutes. Turn on broiler, and broil chicken until it sizzles and turns golden brown and juices no longer run. Remove from oven and let sit for 5 minutes before serving.

Orange Sweet Potatoes – serves 10

10 large sweet potatoes

1½ teaspoons salt

zest and juice from 3 oranges

5 tablespoons butter

Peel sweet potatoes, cut into 1-inch cubes, and place in large sauce pan. Cover with salted water. Bring to a boil; then reduce heat to simmer. Cover and cook for 10–12 minutes or until fork tender. Drain. Add orange juice, zest, butter, and 1½ teaspoons salt. Beat with electric mixer until potatoes are light and fluffy. (Use hand potato masher if you like your potatoes lumpy!) Serve immediately.

Garlic-Roasted Green Beans with Shallots and Hazelnuts – serves 12

15 medium shallots

3 pounds green beans, trimmed

15 medium garlic cloves, coarsely chopped

9 tablespoons extra-virgin olive oil

3 teaspoons kosher salt

$1\frac{1}{2}$ teaspoons freshly ground pepper

$\frac{3}{4}$ cup finely chopped fresh Italian parsley

$\frac{3}{4}$ cup coarsely chopped toasted hazelnuts

3 teaspoons finely grated lemon zest

Position rack mid-oven and preheat to 450°F. Slice each shallot lengthwise into $\frac{1}{4}$-inch slices. Put the shallots, green beans, and garlic in a bowl. Toss with oil, sprinkle with salt and pepper, and toss again. Transfer to a 10 x 15" glass baking dish and roast 18–20 minutes until tender and very lightly browned, stirring ONCE. Combine parsley, hazelnuts, and lemon zest in a small bowl. Sprinkle the parsley mixture over the vegetables and toss to coat. Serve immediately.

Chocolate Spice Cake with Chocolate Fudge Frosting – serves 10–12

Frosting

12 ounces semisweet chocolate chips

$1\frac{3}{4}$ cups heavy cream

3 tablespoons unsalted butter, room temperature

1 tablespoon corn syrup

Prepare an ice bath and set aside. Place chocolate chips in the bowl of a food processor and pulse until roughly chopped. Combine cream, butter, and corn syrup in a small saucepan. Bring to a boil over medium heat, stirring constantly until butter is melted. With the motor running, pour this cream mixture through the feed tube of the food processor and process until completely smooth, about 2 minutes. Transfer frosting to a bowl and set over the ice bath. Stir every 10 minutes, until frosting is thick but still spreadable.

Chocolate Spice Cake

unsalted butter and all-purpose flour, to coat baking dish

1 tablespoon fresh ginger, grated

¼ cup water

½ cup dried cranberries

¼ cup golden raisins

1 cup all-purpose flour

¼ cup cocoa powder

¾ teaspoon baking powder

¼ teaspoon baking soda

¼ teaspoon salt

1 tablespoon ground ginger

1 cup (2 sticks) unsalted butter, room temperature

1 cup sugar

2 large eggs

1 teaspoon pure vanilla extract

1 cup sour cream

Preheat the oven to 350°F. Butter and flour a 6-cup Bundt pan and set aside. Place the grated ginger, water, cranberries, and raisins in a small saucepan and bring to a boil. Reduce to simmer and cook until liquid has evaporated—about 5 minutes. Set aside to cool. In a medium bowl, sift together the flour, cocoa, baking powder, baking soda, salt, and ground ginger and set aside. Place the butter and sugar in bowl. Whisk until light and fluffy, 2–3 minutes. Add the eggs one at time, beating well after each addition. Stir in the vanilla. Add the flour mixture and sour cream in alternate batches, starting and ending with the flour mixture. Beat just until combined. Fold in the dried fruit mixture. Pour the batter into the prepared pan and bake for 40–50 minutes or until a cake tester inserted into center comes out clean. Remove from the oven, transfer to a wire rack, and let cake cool in the pan for 30 minutes. Invert the cake onto a wire rack to cool completely.

Place cake on a cake plate or serving platter, and apply a thick coating of chocolate fudge frosting. Slice generously.

Monday – Day Two
Continental Breakfast

English Muffins, Bagels, Cream Cheese, Fruit Jam,
Orange Juice, Fresh Melon Slices, Yogurt, Granola,
and Coffee and Tea

Lunch

Yucatan-Style Chicken, Lime, and Orzo Soup
Warm Flour Tortillas
Butter Lettuce with Creamy Dijon Dressing
Brownies and Chilled Grapes

Yucatan-Style Chicken, Lime, and Orzo Soup – serves 12

2¼ cups orzo

4½ tablespoons olive oil

3 medium white onions, thinly sliced

6 jalapeño chiles, thinly sliced

19 garlic cloves, thinly sliced

2¼ pounds skinless, boneless chicken breasts,
  cut into matchstick-size strips

15 cups chicken broth

1 cup fresh lime juice

3 large tomatoes, seeded and chopped

¾ cup chopped fresh cilantro

salt and pepper to taste

fresh cilantro sprigs, for garnish

Cook orzo in pot of boiling salted water until just tender. Drain and rinse well. Heat oil in large saucepan over medium heat. Add onion and chiles. Sauté until onion begins to caramelize, about 15 minutes; add garlic and sauté for additional 2–3 minutes, being careful not to let the garlic burn. Add chicken and sauté 1 minute. Add broth, lime juice, and tomatoes. Simmer until chicken is cooked through, about 3 minutes. Mix in orzo, then chopped cilantro. Season soup with salt and pepper.

Ladle soup into bowls. Garnish with cilantro sprigs and flank with warm flour tortillas.

Creamy Dijon Dressing

makes 1 cup

½ cup mayonnaise

½ cup extra-virgin olive oil

6 tablespoons Dijon mustard

4 tablespoons champagne or white wine vinegar

salt and pepper to taste

Whisk first four ingredients together in a small bowl and season with salt and pepper. Cover, chill, and keep in refrigerator for up to 5 days.

Brownies – makes 24

shortening and flour, to coat baking dish

1 cup butter

4 squares unsweetened baking chocolate

3 teaspoons ground cinnamon

4 large eggs

2 cups sugar

2 teaspoons vanilla

1½ cups flour

1 teaspoon baking powder

1 teaspoon baking soda

½ teaspoon salt

1 cup chopped nuts (optional)

Preheat oven to 350°F. Coat 13 x 9 x 2" baking dish with vegetable shortening and flour. Shake to get rid of excess flour. Melt butter, chocolate, and cinnamon in medium saucepan over low heat. Remove and let cool. In large bowl, beat eggs and sugar until light and fluffy. Add chocolate mixture and vanilla and stir to blend well. Add flour, baking powder, baking soda, and salt. Stir until well blended. Fold in nuts if desired. Pour thick batter into prepared dish and bake for 25 minutes or until toothpick inserted into the middle of the brownies comes out clean.

It's nice to serve bunches of chilled grapes alongside these rich brownies.

Dinner

Rolled Green Chile Enchiladas

Warm Flour Tortillas

Mocha Cake

Rolled Green Chile Enchiladas – serves 10

Three separate items go into making this recipe: green chile sauce, guacamole, and the enchiladas themselves.

Green Chile Sauce*

1 16-ounce package frozen, chopped green chiles, thawed

1 small white onion, thinly sliced

2 garlic cloves, thinly sliced

2 tablespoons butter

1 14-ounce can fire-roasted, diced tomatoes or 6 Roma tomatoes, coarsely diced and roasted in 350°F oven for 45 minutes

salt and butter to taste

Thaw green chile and pour into medium sauce pot. Sauté onion and garlic cloves in small sauté pan, with butter, over medium-low heat for 30 minutes or until they begin to caramelize. Add onion-garlic mixture to green chile, add tomatoes, and bring to a boil. Immediately turn heat to medium-low and simmer for 1 hour. Remove from heat. Let cool to room temperature, cover, and refrigerate.

* Will last up to 2 weeks in refrigerator. Can be served with your favorite wheat-flour tortillas, warmed in the oven.

Enchiladas

1 teaspoon vegetable oil

Green Chile Sauce (above)

2 dozen fresh yellow or white corn tortillas

2 pounds asadero cheese

1 head iceberg lettuce, chopped

Fresh diced tomatoes to taste

Preheat oven to 350°F. Lightly oil sides and bottom of a large 9 x 12" baking dish. Heat green chile over medium-low until it begins to simmer. Remove from heat and cover. Wrap tortillas in clean, damp dishtowel and microwave on high for 1 minute. Set aside. Coarsely grate ½ pound of the cheese and set aside. Cut the remaining 1½ pounds of cheese into ½-inch strips. Wrap each strip of cheese with a warm tortilla and place in baking dish with the rolled edge on the bottom. Continue with the cheese and tortillas, placing rolled tortillas closely together, until all the tortillas have been used. Pour warm green chile over tortillas and sprinkle with grated cheese. Cover baking dish tightly with foil and heat in oven for 15 minutes. Remove foil and continue to heat until cheese on top begins to turn golden and bubbles. Remove from oven.

Place two enchiladas on each plate. Garnish with chopped iceberg lettuce topped with fresh, diced tomatoes and a dollop of guacamole. Flank with warm flour tortillas.

Guacamole – makes 2½ cups

2 large avocados, firm but ripe

¼ cup grated onion

1 cup finely chopped seeded tomatoes

1 jalapeño, seeded and finely chopped

2 garlic cloves, minced

2 tablespoons fresh lemon juice

salt and pepper to taste

Blend all ingredients together with a large fork in glass or ceramic bowl. Cover with plastic wrap, making sure that it covers the surface of the guacamole to keep it from turning brown. Refrigerate.

Serve with chips or use as garnish for enchiladas.

Mocha Cake – serves 9

1 12-ounce package chocolate chips

2 tablespoons water

2 tablespoons instant coffee

2 tablespoons sugar

6 eggs, separated

1 teaspoon vanilla

1 package chocolate wafers, finely crushed

Melt first four ingredients in double boiler, stirring often. Let cool. Beat egg yolks into chocolate mixture. Add vanilla. Beat the egg whites until stiff but not dry. Fold chocolate mixture and egg whites together. Layer chocolate wafer crumbs and chocolate mixture into 8" square pan, beginning and ending with crumbs— 5 layers. Freeze at least 1 hour, then refrigerate.

Top with dollop of whipped cream sprinkled with cocoa powder.

Tuesday – Day Three
Breakfast

Spinach Quiche with Sun-Dried Tomatoes

and Green Chile

Bacon

Fresh Berry Bowl

Spinach Quiche with Sun-Dried Tomatoes and Green Chile

Pie Crust – makes four 9-inch crusts*

4 cups all-purpose flour

2 teaspoons sugar

1 teaspoon sea salt

1¾ cups plus 2 tablespoons solid vegetable shortening

1 large egg

2 tablespoons champagne vinegar

1 tablespoon water

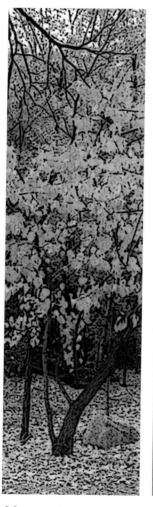

Place the flour, sugar, and salt in a large bowl. Add shortening and mix with a fork until crumbly. In separate bowl, mix the egg, vinegar, and water. Add the egg mixture to the flour mixture and combine until the flour is moistened. Divide into 4 portions, shaping each into a disk. Wrap each disc in plastic and refrigerate at least 30 minutes before rolling out.

*I like to make as many as I can in advance! These pie crusts can be refrigerated up to 1 week or frozen up to 1 month. Defrost the crust overnight in the refrigerator before rolling out.

Quiche – makes two 9-inch quiches, serves 10

2 large eggs, well beaten

6 large eggs

1½ cups 1% milk

1½ cups heavy cream or half and half

⅔ teaspoon dry mustard

¼ teaspoon nutmeg

salt and pepper

6 scallions, white and light green parts thinly sliced

1 cup packaged, sun-dried tomatoes, slightly chopped

1 cup chopped fresh or frozen green chiles

3 cups baby spinach leaves, stems removed, lightly packed

20 ounces grated gruyere cheese

shaved parmesan cheese (optional)

Preheat oven to 400°F. Roll out two pie crusts to fit two 9" pie tins with a ½-inch overhang. Fold overhang in toward center of pie crust and pinch together. Pierce sides and bottom of crusts with fork. Brush inside crust with the 2 beaten eggs and pour whatever is left of eggs into a medium-size mixing bowl. Add remaining 6 eggs, milk, cream, dry mustard, nutmeg, salt, and pepper. Whisk well and set aside. Sprinkle scallions evenly on bottom of both pie crusts. Top each one with half of the sun-dried tomatoes, green chiles, spinach leaves, and gruyere cheese. Pour half of whisked egg mixture over ingredients in each pie tin. Sprinkle parmesan cheese over top. Immediately place pie tins in oven and bake for 15 minutes. Reduce heat to 350°F and bake for another 30–35 minutes or until egg mixture is firm and top of quiche is golden brown. Remove from oven and let cool 15 minutes before serving. Cut each quiche into 5 hearty wedges.

May be served warm or at room temperature. Crisp bacon slices and small bowls of fresh berries make tasty complements to this rich quiche.

Lunch

Smoked Turkey and Gouda Sandwiches
with Orange Mayonnaise
Potato Chips, Cookies, and Apples

Smoked Turkey and Gouda Sandwiches – makes 10

20 slices hearty wheat bread

40 slices good quality smoked turkey

40 slices thinly sliced gouda cheese

40 slices crisply cooked bacon

2 English cucumbers, thinly sliced

20 leaves romaine lettuce

Lay out bread slices and coat well with orange mayonnaise. Layer 2 pieces of turkey on one slice of bread and top with 4 cucumber slices. On second slice of bread, layer cheese, top with 2 bacon slices, and cover with 2 folded romaine leaves. Press both pieces of bread together to form thick sandwich. Cut diagonally in half and use toothpick in each half to keep sandwich together.

Serve these sandwiches with potato chips, cookies, and apples.

Orange Mayonnaise – makes 2¾ cups

1 cup frozen orange concentrate, thawed

2 cups mayonnaise

Pour thawed orange concentrate in shallow skillet and simmer over low heat until reduced to ¾ cup, about 15 minutes. Let cool. Mix orange juice with mayonnaise in small mixing bowl and whisk until well blended. Cover bowl and refrigerate overnight.

Dinner

On Tuesdays, the custom is

for the president of the School to take

the seminar participants out to dinner

at one of Santa Fe's many fine restaurants.

In the fall, they are just in time

to hear the town heave a big sigh of relief after

the busy summer tourist season.

Wednesday – Day Four
Breakfast

German Oven Pancakes with Mixed-Berry Compote

Sausage

Fresh Fruit Bowl

German Oven Pancakes – serves 10

2 tablespoons butter

2 cups flour

2 tablespoons sugar

2½ cups whole milk

4 large eggs, room temperature

½ teaspoon salt

Preheat oven to 375°F. Put 1 tablespoon butter in each of two glass pie pans. Set aside. Just before mixing the remaining ingredients, put the pie pans into the oven and let the butter melt. Remove pans from oven, and carefully swirl butter to cover their bottoms and sides. Mix flour, sugar, milk, eggs, and salt together in large mixing bowl. It will be a thin batter. Pour immediately into hot, butter-coated pie pans and return to oven. Bake for 30 minutes. Dough will puff up, like a popover, but will sink back down as it cools. Cut into 5 wedges per pan and place on individual plates immediately.

Sprinkle with powdered sugar and serve warm with a side of warm mixed-berry compote.

Mixed-Berry Compote – makes 2½ cups

2 cups frozen berries

½ cup orange juice

2 teaspoons fresh lemon juice

1 teaspoon lemon zest

¾ cup sugar

Place ingredients in heavy saucepan. Slowly bring to boil, stirring occasionally. Reduce heat and let simmer for 40 minutes until sauce thickens.

Pour into small pitcher and serve warm. Sausages make a good savory companion to the sweet fruit and the pancakes.

Fresh Fruit Bowl

Using whatever fresh fruit is available, cut into bite-size pieces and put into individual 6-ounce ramekins.

Serve with a slice of fresh lime or lemon.

Lunch

Chinese Chicken Noodle Soup
with Sesame and Green Onion
Baby Spinach Salad with Pears
Fruit Sorbet

Chinese Chicken Noodle Soup with Sesame and Green Onion – serves 6

1 pound skinless, boneless chicken breast halves, cut lengthwise into thin strips

3 tablespoons soy sauce

2 tablespoons dry sherry

2 tablespoons oriental sesame oil

3 garlic cloves, minced

3 tablespoons tahini

2 tablespoons minced, peeled fresh ginger

1 tablespoon seasoned rice vinegar

1 tablespoon sugar

1½ teaspoons chili-garlic sauce

4 cups chopped Napa cabbage (about 1 head)

6 green onions, thinly sliced

8 cups canned, low-salt chicken broth

1 14-ounce package fresh yakisoba noodles, cut into 2½-inch strips

½ cup fresh cilantro, chopped

Stir chicken, soy sauce, sherry, and 1 tablespoon sesame oil in medium bowl to blend. Let stand 20 minutes or refrigerate up to 2 hours. Whisk garlic, tahini, ginger, vinegar, sugar, and chili-garlic sauce in small bowl. Heat remaining tablespoon of sesame oil in heavy pot over medium-high heat. Add cabbage and green onions and sauté until cabbage is tender, about 5 minutes. Add broth and bring to boil. Add chicken with marinade and tahini-garlic mixture. Reduce heat to low and simmer until chicken is cooked through, about 5 minutes.*

Cook noodles in large pot of boiling, salted water. Cook according to package directions (do not overcook). Drain and rinse with cool water twice to remove starch.

Spoon noodles into individual bowls. Add half of cilantro to hot soup pot and gently stir. Pour hot soup over noodles in individual bowls. Sprinkle remaining cilantro onto each bowl and serve immediately.

A cup of fruit sorbet tastes good after this flavorful soup.

* This part of the recipe can be made 1 day ahead. Let it cool slightly and refrigerate. Bring to a simmer before serving.

Baby Spinach Salad with Pears – serves 10

2 small packages fresh baby spinach leaves

5 Bosque pears

paprika

Rinse and stem spinach leaves. Wash pears, core, and cut into bite-size pieces. Place handful of spinach leaves on each plate, distribute pear pieces evenly among all plates, and sprinkle pears with paprika for color. Serve immediately, as pears will turn brown quickly.

Dinner

Roasted Salmon with Red Pepper and Corn Relish
Carrot Rice Pilaf (Gajar Pullau)
Quick Loaf Cake with Spiked Fruit Coulis

Roasted Salmon with Red Pepper and Corn Relish – serves 10

Before preparing the relish and salmon, toast 2 tablespoons plus 2 teaspoons of coriander seeds in a small skillet over medium heat until aromatic, stirring frequently, about 2 minutes. Cool slightly. Crush in mortar with pestle.

Relish

1 tablespoon plus 1 teaspoon toasted and crushed coriander seeds

4 red bell peppers

4 tablespoons extra-virgin olive oil

4 cups fresh corn kernels (about 4 ears)

4 green onions, thinly sliced

3 garlic cloves, minced

2 tablespoons chopped fresh thyme

$\frac{1}{4}$ cup dry white wine

2 tablespoons fresh lemon juice

1 tablespoon honey

$\frac{1}{4}$ cup fresh Italian parsley, chopped

Char peppers over gas flame or under broiler until blackened on all sides. Put in paper bag for 10 minutes. Peel and seed, then cut into $\frac{1}{2}$-inch pieces. Set aside. Heat 2 tablespoons oil in heavy large skillet over medium-high heat. Add corn and green onions and sauté until corn begins to brown in spots. Add garlic and thyme, sauté 2 minutes. Add wine and stir until liquid evaporates, then remove from heat. Stir in bell peppers, lemon juice, honey, and remaining 2 tablespoons olive oil. Add $1\frac{1}{2}$ teaspoons toasted and crushed coriander seeds.*

Stir parsley into relish. Season to taste with salt and pepper.

*Relish can be made to this point 8 hours ahead. Cover and refrigerate. Stir over medium heat until heated through before adding parsley and seasoning.

Salmon

1 tablespoon plus 1 teaspoon toasted and crushed
   coriander seeds

$\frac{1}{4}$ cup extra-virgin olive oil

$\frac{1}{4}$ cup fresh lemon juice

2 tablespoons honey

2 tablespoons paprika

2 teaspoons salt

10 5–6-ounce skinless salmon fillets ($1\frac{3}{4}$ inches thick)

Preheat oven to 400°F. Line large baking sheet with foil. Mix toasted and crushed coriander seeds, oil, lemon juice, honey, paprika, and salt in medium bowl. Brush salmon all over with mixture. Transfer to prepared baking sheet. Roast salmon until opaque in center, about 10 minutes.

Transfer to platter. Spoon relish over salmon and serve.

Carrot Rice Pilaf (Gajar Pullau) – serves 10

$1\frac{1}{2}$ cups basmati rice

2 tablespoons butter

1 cup peeled and grated carrot

$3\frac{1}{2}$ cups water

2 2-inch cinnamon sticks

$\frac{2}{3}$ teaspoon salt

Wash the rice in cool water until the water becomes clear. In a large pot, melt butter and sauté the carrot and rice briefly, about 3 minutes. Add water, cinnamon sticks, and salt. Bring to a boil and continue boiling over medium heat for 3 minutes. Reduce heat to low, cover, and simmer for 25 minutes (do not remove pot lid). Remove from heat and let sit undisturbed for at least 10 minutes.

Just before serving, gently fluff with fork.

Spiked Fruit Coulis –

makes 2 cups*

1 1-pound bag frozen, unsweetened berries or fruit

1 cup plus 2 tablespoons semi-dry white wine (e.g., Chenin Blanc)

4–6 tablespoons sugar

3 cloves

2 small bay leaves

¼ teaspoon allspice

1 teaspoon brandy

Process thawed berries, wine, and 4–6 tablespoons sugar until puréed. Pour into medium saucepan. Add cloves, bay leaves, and allspice. Bring to simmer, stirring occasionally. Reduce heat, cover, and simmer 8 minutes. Strain purée into medium bowl and whisk in brandy. Taste, and add more sugar if needed.

*Can be stored, covered, in the refrigerator for a week. Re-whisk before using.

Quick Loaf Cake with Spiked Fruit Coulis – serves 10–14

Quick Loaf Cake – makes 2 loaves*

1 package yellow cake mix

¼ cup sugar

½ cup flour

1 cup sour cream

½ cup vegetable or canola oil

⅔ cup water

4 eggs

2 tablespoons grated lemon rind (optional)

Preheat oven to 375°F. Grease and flour 2 glass loaf pans. Mix all ingredients together in large bowl and, using an electric, hand-held beater, beat for 4 minutes on medium. Pour batter evenly into the two prepared loaf pans and bake 40–45 minutes or until tester toothpick comes out clean. Remove from oven and place on cooling racks for 15 minutes. Run knife around sides of loaf pans, invert, and unmold cakes. Let cool to room temperature, upside down. Wrap in plastic wrap and refrigerate until 2 hours before ready to serve.

*This cake is delicious with any kind of fruit compote or sauce.

Thursday – Day Five
Breakfast

Sally's Breakfast Egg Dish

Bacon

Fresh Fruit Bowl

Sally's Breakfast Egg Dish – serves 10

10 large eggs

1 tablespoon baking powder

1 16-ounce container cottage cheese

½ cup melted butter, cooled to room temperature

½ cup flour

¼ teaspoon nutmeg

½ teaspoon salt

pepper to taste

1 pound monterey jack cheese, grated

1 cup fresh or frozen chopped green chiles

Preheat oven to 350°F. Beat eggs until fluffy and lemon-colored. Add all other ingredients. Fold together until well blended. Pour mixture into greased 9 x 13" baking dish. Bake for 40 minutes or until golden brown. Let sit for 10 minutes before serving.

Serve with Salsa Fresca (see page 180) and crisp slices of bacon.

Fresh Fruit Bowl

Using whatever fresh fruit is available, cut into bite-size pieces and put into individual 6-ounce ramekins. Serve with a slice of fresh lime or lemon.

Lunch

Spinach Pockets

Waldorf Salad

Lemon Bars

Spinach Pockets – serves 4

¼ cup lemon juice

¼ cup water

1 garlic clove, thinly sliced

1 teaspoon kosher salt

1 pound spinach leaves

1 1-pound package phyllo dough, defrosted (12 sheets)

3 tablespoons unsalted butter, melted

½ cup freshly grated parmesan cheese

½ cup ricotta cheese

2 scallions, trimmed and thinly sliced

1 egg

¼ teaspoon kosher salt

¼ teaspoon fresh pepper

In a skillet, combine lemon juice, water, garlic, and salt. Add spinach. Bring to a simmer and cook just until spinach is wilted. Drain. (This can be served as a separate side dish.)

Heat oven to 400°F. In a large bowl, combine the spinach, parmesan, ricotta, scallions, egg, salt, and pepper. Mix well and set aside. Fold 1 sheet of phyllo in half, crosswise, and place on a lightly greased baking sheet. Brush the top with some of the butter. Top with another folded sheet and brush with more butter. Repeat one more time. Leaving a 2-inch border around the edges, place a quarter of the spinach mixture at the end of the pastry. Roll up the pastry, tucking in the sides. Brush with more butter. Repeat to make 3 more pockets. Bake in the oven until puffed and golden, about 30 minutes.

Lemon Bars – makes 9

1 cup plus 2 teaspoons flour

¼ cup powdered sugar

½ cup butter, room temperature

2 medium eggs, well beaten

1 cup sugar

½ teaspoon salt

½ teaspoon baking powder

juice and zest of large lemon

¾ of a 12.5-ounce package sweetened, flaked coconut

Preheat oven to 350°F. Mix 1 cup flour, powdered sugar, and butter as you would a pie crust in a small bowl, using a fork or pastry blender. Gently pat crust into 8 x 8" glass baking dish. Bake for 15 minutes, then remove from oven. While crust is cooking, beat eggs until light and fluffy. Stir in sugar, salt, the remaining 2 teaspoons of flour, and baking powder. Add lemon juice and rind. Fold in coconut and pour batter over crust. Bake 30 minutes or until lemon topping begins to brown around edges. Cool completely and cut into 9 squares.

Serve with chilled grapes.

Waldorf Salad –

serves 10

5 Granny Smith apples, peeled, cored, and cut into bite-size pieces

2 celery stalks, cut in half lengthwise, then on a sharp diagonal

2 cups coarsely chopped cashews

1 cup mayonnaise

¼ cup fresh orange juice

2 tablespoons honey

2 tablespoons mild chile powder

salt and pepper to taste

Cut apples, celery, and nuts, and place in mixing bowl. In separate bowl, whisk together the mayonnaise, orange juice, honey, and chile powder until well blended. Pour over apple mixture and toss to coat. Refrigerate until ready to serve.

Garnish with sprig of parsley.

Dinner

Fiesta Flank Steak

Roasted Red Potatoes with Chives

Jicama-Radish Slaw in Sherry-Shallot Vinaigrette

Broiled Apples with Vanilla Ice Cream

Fiesta Flank Steak – serves 6

8 garlic cloves, thinly sliced

4 shallots, sliced

¾ cup plus 1 tablespoon
   canola oil

2 pounds beef flank steak

½ zucchini

½ yellow squash

½ eggplant

½ pound spinach, cleaned
   and stemmed

2 carrots, finely diced

1 teaspoon sea salt

freshly ground black pepper
   to taste

In a small bowl, mix together the garlic, the shallots, and ½ cup oil. Place the flank steak in a shallow bowl, and drizzle the oil mixture over the steak. Cover the dish with plastic wrap and place in the refrigerator for at least 6 hours, turning the meat over once.

Trim the ends of the zucchini, squash, and eggplant. Cut off the peel, with ½ inch of flesh. Cut the peeled pieces into ¼-inch slices and then into small dice. In a medium sauté pan, heat 1 tablespoon oil, and sauté the spinach over medium heat until wilted, about 2 minutes. Let cool to room temperature; then chop the spinach roughly and place in a medium bowl. In the same sauté pan, add 1 tablespoon oil, and cook the carrots for 2–3 minutes over medium heat until just tender. Place the carrots with the spinach. Reheat the pan to medium-hot with 1 tablespoon oil, and add the squashes, cooking until just tender, about 3 minutes. Transfer to the bowl of spinach and carrots. Heat the remaining 2 tablespoons oil to hot, and add the eggplant, cooking until tender, about 3–4 minutes. Add to the rest of the vegetables and toss together with salt and pepper.

Preheat oven to 400°F. Drain the marinated beef, place it on a cutting board, and cover it with a sheet of plastic wrap. Save the garlic and shallots. Using a mallet or rolling pin, pound the steak on both sides until it is about ¼ to ½ inch thick throughout. Season with salt and pepper. Place the drained garlic and shallots from the marinade and two cups of the vegetable mixture down the center of the meat lengthwise, lightly season with salt and pepper, and roll the meat lengthwise, tying with kitchen string about every 2 inches. Generously season the rolled steak with salt and coarse pepper. Place the stuffed steak in a baking dish, and roast it for 16–18 minutes for medium rare. Remove from the oven to a cutting board and let rest for 10–15 minutes before slicing. Cut the meat in thick slices and place on individual plates. Serve immediately.

Roasted Red Potatoes with Chives – serves 12

3 pounds small, new red potatoes (about 30), scrubbed

kosher salt and freshly ground pepper

9 tablespoons olive oil

1½ cups freshly grated parmigiano reggiano

3 tablespoons thinly sliced fresh chives

Position rack mid-oven and preheat to 450°F. Cook potatoes: start with cold water just to cover, and add 3 teaspoons salt. Bring to boil over high heat, then lower to a gentle simmer. Cook until tender when pierced with fork, about 15–20 minutes. Drain and let cool slightly. Oil the bottom of a glass baking dish. Put the potatoes in the dish, piercing each with fork tines, twisting slightly to break the skin a bit. Gently squeeze the sides of each potato to make it pop open slightly (like a baked potato). Season the potatoes generously with salt and pepper. Drizzle the remaining 6 tablespoons oil over the potatoes and sprinkle with cheese. Roast until the potatoes are golden brown and crisp, about 25–30 minutes. Sprinkle with chives and serve immediately.

Jicama-Radish Slaw – serves 10

1 large jicama

2 bunches small
   red radishes, washed, with
   stems and tips removed

juice of $\frac{1}{2}$ lemon

$\frac{1}{2}$ teaspoon fine lemon zest

$1\frac{1}{2}$ teaspoons olive oil

1 teaspoon rice vinegar

1 scallion, white and pale
   green part only, thinly
   sliced

Peel jicama with potato peeler. Cut in quarters and thinly slice into matchstick-size pieces. Place in small bowl and cover with cold water. Thinly slice radishes, place in medium mixing bowl, and cover with damp paper towel to keep them from turning brown. Whisk lemon juice and zest, olive oil, and vinegar in small bowl until well blended. Drain jicama and mix in with radishes. Add sliced scallion; then pour lemon mixture over vegetables. Gently toss to cover evenly.

Scoop a generous, soup spoon–size dollop of slaw over a bed of baby spinach or other fresh salad greens of your choice. Serve immediately.

Broiled Apples – serves 8

6 sweet, firm apples (Rome
   Beauties or Empires),
   peeled, cored, and cut into
   8–10 wedges

$\frac{1}{3}$ cup fresh lemon juice

4 tablespoons butter, melted

$\frac{3}{4}$ cup sugar

$\frac{1}{3}$ cup rum or $\frac{1}{2}$ cup maple
   syrup

2 pints vanilla ice cream

Turn on broiler. Toss the apples with the lemon juice, butter, and all but 2 tablespoons of the sugar.* Arrange on a baking sheet in a single layer. Broil the apples about 8 inches from the heat for 8–10 minutes or until tender. Sprinkle with the remaining 2 tablespoons of sugar and broil until melted. Meanwhile, heat the rum or maple syrup in a small saucepan over low heat.

Serve the warm apples over French vanilla ice cream. Drizzle with warm syrup.

Sherry Shallot Vinaigrette –
makes $1\frac{1}{2}$ cups

$\frac{1}{4}$ cup finely diced
   shallots (4 large)

$\frac{3}{4}$ teaspoon sea salt

$\frac{1}{3}$ cup sherry
   vinegar

1 cup extra-virgin
   olive oil

black pepper to
   taste

Whisk the shallots, salt, and vinegar together until salt is dissolved. Slowly whisk in the oil until well blended. Season with pepper.

Serve over fresh mixed greens alongside the Jicama Radish Slaw.

*Can be made to this point up to 1 day ahead. Store in airtight container and refrigerate.

Friday – Day Six
(Farewell)
Continental Breakfast

Bagels, Cream Cheese, Jam,

English Muffins,

Granola, Yogurt,

Hardboiled Eggs,

Juice, Coffee and Tea

Autumn burned brightly,
a running flame
through the mountains,
a torch flung to the trees.
                    —Faith Baldwin

Winter

I prefer winter and fall,
when you feel the bone structure
of the landscape—the loneliness of it,
the dead feeling of winter.
Something waits beneath it,
the whole story doesn't show.

—Andrew Wyeth

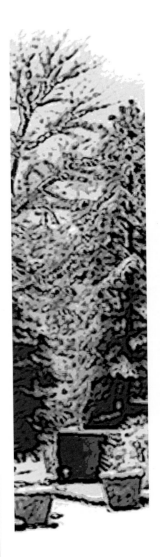

When Santa Fe's aspens shed the last of their golden leaves and the startling oranges and reds of the scrub oaks fade, the city swirls the fine, white cloak of winter around its shoulders and is transformed by sparkling hues of ice and snow—blinding whites and subtle lavenders stained blue with shadows blur the outlines of the adobe-style buildings. Trees stand proud and stark, displaying their bones against the azure skies of mostly sunny days. The holiday season brings its own warm glow as farolitos—paper bags filled with sand and illuminated by candles—outline walls, roofs, driveways, and sidewalks. An inhalation of sharp, crisp air carries a hint of pine, cedar smoke, and cinnamon and the rich aromas of posole, Chamayan chiles, stews, and tamales. Brisk winter walks evoke thoughts of hot food and drink, feasts, and gatherings of colleagues, friends, and family.

Outside town, there are still plenty of mule deer to be seen, and December is a particularly good time to spot coyotes, as the "grey ghosts" are lured closer by the smells of food. The spillway at Cochiti Dam is the perfect place to watch bald eagles wintering in its shadow, roosting in the cottonwoods, cruising the skies. Even on warmer days, winter hikes can bring thrilling surprises: a herd of a hundred elk in the vast caldera beyond Los Alamos, the last of the sandhill cranes or honking vees of snow geese headed toward the Las Vegas National Wildlife Refuge and points farther south. At the School for Advanced Research, a new group of seminarians breathes deeply and prepares to pursue fresh insights by sharing their research with one another in front of the piñon fires in the Seminar House's cozy living room.

WELCOME DINNER
Saturday

Gypsy Stew

Green Salad with Pears and Walnuts

Apple Crisp

Green Salad with Pears and Walnuts –
serves 10

1 cup walnuts, toasted

2 heads of red-leaf lettuce, washed

5 D'anjou pears, cut into wedges

Preheat oven to 400°F. Place walnuts on rimmed baking sheet and bake until aromatic, about 10 minutes. Watch carefully so that they do not burn. Remove from oven and set aside. Wash lettuce and tear into bite-size pieces. Place on plates. Arrange ½ pear into a loose fan shape on top of lettuce. Sprinkle each salad with walnuts.

Gypsy Stew – serves 10–12

1 3-pound whole chicken, plus 4–5 extra breast halves

6 yellow onions, peeled and cut into eighths

25 garlic cloves, peeled and halved

1 quart dry cocktail sherry, divided

1 16-ounce can chicken broth or stock

32 ounces frozen, whole green chiles

2 24-ounce cans whole, fire-roasted tomatoes

2 teaspoons salt

1 pound monterey jack cheese, cut into ½-inch cubes

Put chicken, onions, garlic, half of the sherry, and broth into a large, heavy soup pot (if there isn't enough broth to cover the ingredients, add water or more broth). Cover pot and simmer slowly for 1–1½ hours or until chicken is cooked. Cut thawed chiles into 2-inch chunks. Using two forks, tear tomatoes apart and place in large bowl with chiles and all the juices, to mingle while the chicken is cooking. Remove cooked chicken from pot and carefully place in colander to cool enough to pick meat off the bones. Add chiles, tomatoes, remaining sherry, salt, and chicken pieces to stock. Cover and simmer slowly for an hour. MAKE SURE IT DOES NOT BOIL, as this will make the sherry boil off, but undercooking will leave the broth bitter.

Place cheese cubes in the bottom of individual serving bowls. Ladle stew into each bowl (the heat will melt the cheese). Serve with flour tortillas and, if desired, a side of guacamole (page 19).

Apple Crisp – serves 10

10–12 Granny Smith apples, peeled, cored, and cut into eighths

1 cup sugar

½ teaspoon salt

¾ teaspoon cinnamon

¼ teaspoon nutmeg

1 tablespoon lemon juice

½ cup flour

1 cup brown sugar

2 cups rolled oats (not instant)

1 cup coarsely chopped pecans or walnuts

1 tablespoon vanilla

1 cup butter, cut into small cubes

Preheat oven to 350°F. Peel apples; core and cut into 8 wedges. Place in large bowl and mix with sugar, salt, cinnamon, nutmeg, and lemon juice. Mix well to coat apple slices. In separate bowl, mix flour, brown sugar, rolled oats, nuts, and vanilla together. Add butter cubes to flour mixture and, with your fingers, blend until mixture resembles coarse meal (it will be quite lumpy). Pour apples into a 13 x 9" baking pan, and sprinkle butter-flour mixture over them. Place in lower third of your preheated oven and bake until crust turns golden brown and apples begin to bubble, about 45 minutes.

Sunday – Day One
Breakfast

Quiche Lorraine

Healthy Blueberry-Bran Muffins

Fresh Fruit Bowl

Quiche Lorraine –
makes two 9-inch pies, serves 10

Pie Crust
(see page 22)

Quiche

½ pound bacon

¾ cup finely chopped onion

1 pound swiss cheese, cut into small cubes

6 eggs, slightly beaten

4 cups milk

1 teaspoon salt

1 teaspoon freshly ground pepper

⅛ teaspoon nutmeg

Preheat oven to 450°F. Line two 9" pie pans with pie crust. Poke bottom and sides with fork tines and set aside. Fry bacon in large skillet until crisp. Remove from skillet to cool, and pour out all but 1 tablespoon of bacon grease. Reheat skillet and add onion, cooking until golden brown. Remove from skillet and place on paper towel–covered plate to soak up any remaining bacon grease. Dividing evenly, sprinkle crumbled bacon and onion into the bottom of each pie crust. Cover with cheese cubes. Whisk eggs, milk, salt, pepper, and nutmeg together in large bowl until well blended. Pour half of this mixture into the pie shell. Bake 10 minutes. Then reduce heat to 325°F and bake until firm and golden on top, about 35 minutes.

Remove from oven and let sit for 10 minutes before serving. May be served at room temperature.

Healthy Blueberry-Bran Muffins
makes 12–16

1 8-ounce can crushed pineapple, in juice

1 cup All-Bran cereal

¼ cup milk

1 egg, slightly beaten

¼ cup oil

2 tablespoons light molasses

1 cup unbleached flour

⅓ cup sugar

2 teaspoons baking powder

⅓ cup fresh or frozen blueberries

Preheat oven to 400°F. Drain pineapple well, reserving ¼ cup juice. Combine reserved pineapple juice, cereal, and milk in bowl and let sit for 3 minutes to soften cereal. Stir in pineapple, egg, oil, and molasses. Combine flour, sugar, and baking powder in a bowl. Add to pineapple mixture and stir to combine. Gently fold in blueberries. Spoon into paper-lined muffin tins. Bake for 25 minutes or until wooden toothpick comes out clean. Serve warm.

Fresh Fruit Bowl

Using whatever fresh fruit is available, cut into bite-size pieces and put into individual 6-ounce ramekins. Serve with a slice of fresh lime or lemon.

Lunch

Corn Cheddar Chowder

Cream Biscuits

Sliced Cucumbers and Radishes

Karen's Kahlua Cake

Corn Cheddar Chowder – serves 10–12

8 ounces bacon, chopped

¼ cup olive oil

6 cups chopped yellow
   onions (4 large)

5 garlic cloves, chopped

½ stick unsalted butter

½ cup flour

2 teaspoons kosher salt

1 teaspoon freshly ground
   pepper

½ teaspoon ground turmeric

12 cups chicken stock

6 cups white potatoes
   (2 pounds), unpeeled
   and medium-diced

3 pounds frozen, petite corn

2 cups half and half

8 ounces sharp white
   cheddar cheese, grated

In large stockpot over medium-high heat, cook the bacon in the olive oil until the bacon is crisp. Remove with slotted spoon and set aside. Reduce heat to medium, add onions, garlic and butter, and cook until the onions are translucent and limp. Stir in flour, salt, pepper, and turmeric and cook for 3 minutes. Add chicken stock and potatoes and bring to a boil.* Add corn to warm (or re-warmed) soup and bring to gentle simmer. Add half and half and cheese. Cook 5 minutes or until cheese is melted. Season to taste with additional salt and fresh pepper.

Serve hot with garnish of bacon.

Variations

Add 1½ cups well-drained chopped green chiles after potatoes
   have come to a boil.

Or—Add cooked, shredded chicken along with cheese.

Or—Eliminate cream and cheese for a low-fat version.

Or—Any combination above!

*You may stop the process at this point and let sit on stove until 1 hour before serving time.

54   *Winter*

Cream Biscuits – makes 12

2 cups flour

1 teaspoon salt

1 tablespoon baking powder

2 teaspoons sugar

1 to $1\frac{1}{2}$ cups heavy cream

6 tablespoons butter, melted

Preheat oven to 425°F. Combine flour, salt, baking powder, and sugar in a mixing bowl. Stir the ingredients with a fork to blend. Slowly add 1 cup of the cream to the mixture, stirring constantly.

Gather the dough together; when it folds together and feels tender, it is ready to knead.

BUT if it seems dry and pieces are falling away, slowly add enough additional cream to make the dough hold together. Place the dough on a lightly floured board and knead for 1 minute. Pat the dough into a $\frac{1}{2}$-inch-thick square. Cut into 12 squares, and dip each into the melted butter so that all sides are coated. Place the biscuits 2 inches apart on an ungreased cookie sheet. Bake for 15 minutes or until lightly browned. Serve hot.

Sliced Cucumbers and Radishes –
serves 10

2 English cucumbers, unpeeled and thinly sliced

2 bunches red or orange radishes, washed and thinly sliced

2 tablespoons rice wine vinegar

1 tablespoon olive oil

1 teaspoon sea salt

$\frac{1}{2}$ teaspoon freshly ground pepper

Place sliced cucumbers and radishes in medium-size bowl. Add vinegar, olive oil, salt, and pepper. Stir gently to coat vegetables. Cover and refrigerate until ready to serve.

Karen's Kahlua Cake – serves 12–15

1 package chocolate cake mix

1 4-ounce instant chocolate pudding mix

4 eggs

2 cups sour cream

¾ cup vegetable oil

⅓ cup Kahlua

6 ounces chocolate chips

powdered sugar, for dusting

Preheat oven to 350°F. Prepare bunt pan by greasing and flouring the insides. Set aside. Mix first six ingredients together, blending well. Fold in chocolate chips and pour into bunt pan. Tap pan gently on counter to remove air pockets. Bake for 60 minutes. Remove from oven and let cool on rack for 10 minutes. Invert pan and remove cake, placing on serving platter. Dust with powdered sugar and cool completely.

Dust each slice with powdered sugar again before serving.

Dinner

Wine-Baked Halibut Steaks with Mustard-Fennel Butter
Cooked Spinach
Roasted New Potatoes
Banana Fritters with Coconut Sorbet

Wine-Baked Halibut Steaks with Mustard-Fennel Butter – serves 10

5 teaspoons fennel seeds

15 tablespoons unsalted butter, room temperature

¾ cup chopped fresh parsley

8 tablespoons Dijon mustard

10 6–8-ounce halibut steaks

2½ cups dry white wine

salt and pepper to taste

Preheat oven to 400°F. Place rack in middle of oven. Toast fennel seeds in small skillet over medium heat until fragrant, about 5 minutes. Remove from heat and chop seeds. Combine butter, parsley, mustard, and fennel seeds in small bowl. Mash together with back of spoon, blending well to make a paste. Season to taste with salt and pepper. Sprinkle fish with salt and pepper. Place fish in two 9 x 9" baking dishes. Pour wine over fish and bake until fish are opaque in the center, basting occasionally with wine and fish juices, about 15 minutes. Place individual steaks on serving plates, and spread fennel butter over each steak. Serve immediately with a sprig of fresh parsley as a garnish.

Cooked Spinach – serves 10

¾ cup fresh lemon juice

¾ cup water

3 garlic cloves, finely diced

3 teaspoons kosher salt

3 pounds fresh spinach, washed and stemmed

4 tablespoons lemon zest

Combine lemon juice, water, garlic, and salt in large skillet. Bring to a simmer* and add spinach, cooking until spinach is just wilted and still a rich green color. You may have to do this in small batches, removing the cooked spinach with a slotted spoon and placing in a bowl. Keep bowl covered to retain the heat until you are ready to serve. Top each serving with a sprinkle of lemon zest.

*You may also add 1½ cups dried cranberries to the simmering lemon/water mixture.

Roasted New Potatoes – serves 10

5 pounds new potatoes, cut in half

1 cup extra-virgin olive oil

2½ teaspoons coarse salt

6 rosemary sprigs (optional)

pepper to taste

Preheat oven to 400°F. Wash and dry potatoes; cut in half and arrange in a single layer on two large, rimmed baking sheets, cut side up. Drizzle with oil and sprinkle with salt and pepper. If you choose to use the rosemary, break each of the 6 sprigs into three pieces and sprinkle them over the potatoes. Roast 40 minutes or until the potatoes just begin to turn tender, stirring every 15 minutes. Serve hot.

Banana Fritters with Coconut Sorbet – serves 10

½ cup rice flour

⅓ cup flour

3 tablespoons sesame seeds

½ teaspoon salt

⅓ teaspoon baking powder

½ cup (about) cold water

4 large bananas, firm but ripe, cut on the diagonal into ½-inch-thick slices

vegetable oil (for deep frying)

coconut sorbet

powdered sugar

Whisk first five ingredients in large bowl to blend. Whisk in ½ cup cold water; whisk in more water if needed until smooth thick batter forms. Add banana slices and gently stir to coat. Cover and let stand at room temperature for 2 hours. Pour enough oil into heavy saucepan to reach depth of 1½ inches. Heat oil over medium-high until deep-fry thermometer reaches 350°F. Working in batches, add 3–4 coated banana slices to oil and cook until just golden brown (separating fritters), about 4 minutes. Remove from oil using slotted spoon and place on paper towels.

Scoop a generous portion of coconut sorbet into 10 individual bowls. Add the divided fritters, dash with powdered sugar. Serve immediately.

Monday – Day Two
Breakfast

Buttermilk Pancakes

Sausage

Fresh Melon Slices

Buttermilk Pancakes – serves 5

1 cup flour

2 teaspoons baking powder

¼ teaspoon salt

1 egg

1½ cups buttermilk, or more as needed

Mix dry ingredients in large mixing bowl. Add egg and slowly mix in buttermilk, stirring constantly, until batter slowly drips from the spoon. Pour in one-half ladle of batter, per pancake, onto hot skillet and cook until small bubbles appear on top. Gently flip pancake over and cook another few minutes or until golden brown. Remove cooked pancakes and place on oven-proof platter. Cover with dish towel and place in 200°F oven until ready to serve.

Place 3–4 pancakes on each plate with a dollop of butter; serve warmed syrup on the side. Add sausages and slices of melon to complete the meal.

Lunch

Seminar House Scallop Bisque
Butter Lettuce with Citrus Splash
Lemon Sorbet

Seminar House Scallop Bisque – serves 8–10

14 tablespoons unsalted butter

2 cups leeks, white parts only, thinly sliced

1 pound mushroom caps, thinly sliced

⅔ cup Italian parsley, chopped

salt and pepper to taste

6 cups fish stock

2 cups water

2 pounds bay scallops, rinsed several times

½ cup flour

4 eggs

2 cups heavy cream

3 teaspoons pepper flakes or 2 teaspoons chopped chipotle chiles (optional)

1½ cups canned crushed tomatoes

⅔ cup very dry sherry

freshly chopped chives, for garnish

Melt 6 tablespoons butter in heavy soup pot. Add leeks and cook over low heat, covered, for 20 minutes. Add mushrooms and cook gently for 5 minutes or until they begin to render their juices. Add parsley, salt, and pepper, and raise heat. Stir constantly, cooking until mushroom juices disappear. Add fish stock and water to the soup pot and bring to a boil. Reduce heat, cover, and simmer for 15 minutes. Remove from heat, add scallops, and let stand, covered, for 1 minute—no longer, as this will make the scallops tough! Pour the soup through a strainer into a bowl, reserving both the scallop mixture and the broth. Transfer the broth to a smaller saucepan and bring to a boil. Melt the remaining 8 tablespoons of butter in the soup pot. Add flour, stirring constantly, and cook for 5 minutes. Do not let the flour mixture turn brown. Remove from heat and pour in boiling soup stock, beating constantly with a whisk. Turn heat up to medium and simmer for 5 minutes, stirring constantly. Thoroughly mix eggs with cream in a small bowl. Remove soup from heat, and slowly whisk 1 cup of soup into the egg mixture. Whisk this all back into the soup pot. Add pepper flakes and/ or chipotle if desired. Set the soup pot over low heat; stir in tomatoes and sherry. Stir constantly, until soup thickens slightly. DO NOT ALLOW TO BOIL. Add reserved scallop and leek-mushroom mixture and heat for 1 minute. Taste and adjust seasoning to taste. Ladle into warm soup bowls and serve immediately.

Butter Lettuce with Citrus Splash –
makes 10 small side salads

3 heads butter lettuce, washed and dried, torn into bite-size pieces

juice of 1 lime

juice of 1 orange, with pulp

3 teaspoons extra-virgin olive oil

Place lettuce pieces in large bowl. Toss gently with juices and olive oil. Serve immediately.

Lemon sorbet is a nice way to end this meal.

Dinner

Yucatan-Style Pork
Potato Purée with Olive Oil
Roasted Carrots
Raspberry Tart

Yucatan-Style Pork – serves 10

1 3½-pound pork-loin roast

8 ounces pitted prunes

1 tablespoon olive oil

8–10 garlic cloves, peeled

1 large onion, quartered

1 cup apple juice

¼ cup cider vinegar

3 tablespoons chile powder

1 tablespoon salt

1 teaspoon dried oregano

1 cinnamon stick

Preheat oven to 325°F. Using a small sharp knife, make random 1½-inch slits in the pork roast, and stuff each with a prune. Heat the oil in a Dutch oven over medium-high heat, and brown the pork on all sides. Remove the pork from the Dutch oven and set aside. Meanwhile, in a food processor process the garlic until minced. Add the onion and pulse until minced. Add the minced garlic and onion to the Dutch oven and sauté until tender but not browned. Add the apple juice, cider vinegar, chile powder, salt, oregano, and cinnamon. Return the pork to the Dutch oven. Over high heat, bring to a boil. Cover and place in oven. Cook 1½ hours, basting occasionally. Remove the cover and cook 30 minutes longer. Remove the pork from the sauce. Set the sauce aside for 10 minutes. When the fat comes to the surface, skim it off and discard. Boil the sauce over high heat, stirring occasionally, until thickened and reduced to about 1½ cups.

Slice the pork and serve with the sauce.

Potato Purée with Olive Oil – serves 8–10

4 ounces fresh parmesan cheese, shaved

6 pounds medium-size Yukon Gold potatoes

1½ cups half and half

1 cup extra-virgin olive oil

1 tablespoon salt

¾ tablespoon freshly ground pepper

With a vegetable grater, cut the cheese into thin shavings. Set aside. Peel potatoes and cook in large pot of salted water until tender, about 1 hour. Drain potatoes and let cool slightly. Return potatoes to pot and mash with potato masher or large fork. Add half and half; stir over low heat until just warmed. Gradually stir in oil, salt, and pepper. Add half of the parmesan shavings and stir until melted.

Serve on individual plates and top with remaining cheese.

Roasted Carrots – serves 10

15 large carrots, peeled and cut into 2 x ¼" matchsticks

7 tablespoons extra-virgin olive oil

3½ teaspoons sea salt

1 tablespoon coarsely ground pepper

1¼ cups unsalted butter, room temperature

6 tablespoons minced shallots

6 tablespoons finely chopped chives

3 garlic cloves, minced

Preheat oven to 450°F and place rack in middle of oven. Toss the carrots with the olive oil, sprinkle with salt and pepper, and toss again. Transfer to 10 x 15" glass baking dish and roast until the carrots begin to soften, about 30 minutes. Stir occasionally. Combine butter, shallots, chives, and garlic in bowl and blend well with fork. Add the butter to the roasted carrots and toss to coat well. Serve immediately.

Raspberry Tart – serves 10–12

This tart has three separate elements—Pâté Brisée, Lemon Curd, and Almond Cream.

Pâté Brisée

2½ cups all-purpose flour, plus more for dusting

1 teaspoon coarse salt

1 teaspoon sugar

1 cup (2 sticks) unsalted butter, chilled, cut into pieces

¼ to ½ cup ice water

Place flour, salt, and sugar in the bowl of a food processor fitted with the metal blade. Process a few seconds to combine. Add butter pieces and process until mixture resembles coarse meal, about 10 seconds. Add ice water in a slow, steady stream through the feed tube with the machine running, just until dough holds together. Do not process for more than 30 seconds. Turn the dough out onto a plastic wrap–covered work surface. Flatten, and form a disk. Wrap, and refrigerate at least 1 hour before using.

Lemon Curd

¾ cup fresh lemon juice, strained (about 6 lemons)

2 large eggs

3 large egg yolks

½ cup sugar

In the top of double boiler over simmering water, whisk together the lemon juice, eggs, egg yolks, and sugar. Whisk constantly until the mixture thickens, about 15 minutes. Scrape mixture into bowl and lay plastic wrap directly on top of mixture to prevent a skin from forming. Let cool completely. Refrigerate if not using immediately.

Almond Cream

½ cup almond paste

3 tablespoons unsalted butter, at room temperature

½ large beaten egg

½ teaspoon vanilla extract

2 cups fresh raspberries

Cream the almond paste and the butter together with electric beater. Add the egg and vanilla and beat on high until light and fluffy, 4–5 minutes. Refrigerate if not using immediately.

Preheat oven to 350°F. Roll the pâté brisée to ⅛-inch thickness and gently fit into 10" tart pan. Trim the overhang. Spread the almond cream over the bottom of the crust, and bake tart until it is very lightly browned, about 30 minutes. Let cool completely in pan on wire rack. Spread ¾ cup (or more) of the lemon curd over the tart. Cover the surface with a single layer of raspberries —all standing on their stem end. Refrigerate until ready to serve. Best eaten the day it is made.

Tuesday – Day Three
Continental Breakfast

English Muffins, Bagels,

Cream Cheese, Fruit Jam,

Orange Juice,

Fresh Melon Slices,

Yogurt, Granola, and Coffee and Tea

Lunch

Linguine with Chipotle and Red Pepper Sauce

Spring Greens with Bell Pepper Confetti

Garlic Bread

Vanilla Sorbet

Linguine with Chipotle and Red Pepper Sauce – serves 10

6 tablespoons olive oil

3 large red onions, thinly sliced

4 red bell peppers, thinly sliced

⅔ cup dry sherry

2 12-ounce jars roasted red peppers, drained, thinly sliced

4 garlic cloves, minced

4 teaspoons minced, canned chipotle chiles

2 pounds linguine

½ cup chopped fresh parsley

4 tablespoons balsamic vinegar

2 cups freshly grated manchego cheese

Heat olive oil in large skillet over high heat. Add red onions and red bell peppers. Sauté until onions are brown, about 15 minutes. Stir in sherry, roasted red peppers, garlic, and chipotles. Simmer until liquid evaporates, about 6 minutes. Cook linguine until tender but still firm to the bite. Drain and reserve ¼ cup cooking liquid. Return linguine to pot. Add pepper mixture, parsley, vinegar, and reserved ¼ cup liquid. Toss well. Season to taste with salt and pepper. Divide among bowls and top with cheese.

Pair the linguine with garlic bread, and serve a nice French vanilla ice cream or sorbet to finish the meal.

Spring Greens with Bell Pepper Confetti –

serves 10

1 red bell pepper, finely diced

1 orange bell pepper, finely diced

1 yellow bell pepper, finely diced

2 tablespoons extra-virgin olive oil

salt and pepper to taste

24 ounces mixed salad greens

Mix bell peppers together in small bowl and toss with olive oil, salt, and pepper. Divide the greens evenly between the 10 plates, and spoon pepper confetti over the top. Serve immediately.

Dinner

On Tuesdays, the custom is
for the president of the School to take
the seminar participants out to dinner
at one of Santa Fe's many fine restaurants.
Winter's early dusk and the dusting of
high-desert snow make welcome havens
of their fragrant interiors.

Wednesday – Day Four
Breakfast

Grandma Ann's Breakfast Casserole with Ham and Cheese
Berry Oatmeal Coffee Cake
Fresh Fruit

Grandma Ann's Breakfast Casserole with Ham and Cheese – serves 10

8–10 slices whole wheat bread, crusts removed

1 pound diced ham

½ pound American cheese, cut into ½-inch cubes

1 cup frozen, chopped green chiles, thawed and drained (optional)

9 eggs

3 cups milk

½ teaspoon salt

½ teaspoon pepper

½ teaspoon dried mustard

2 cups corn flakes, coarsely crushed

8 tablespoons butter, melted

Fit bread pieces in single layer on bottom of 10 x 12" glass baking pan. Layer ham, cheese (and green chiles, if desired) over the bread slices. Whisk eggs, milk, salt, pepper, and mustard together in large bowl until light and frothy. Pour over bread mixture. Cover with plastic wrap and refrigerate overnight.

Next morning: Preheat oven to 350°F. Remove egg dish from refrigerator. Sprinkle corn flakes over the top, and pour melted butter on top. Bake on middle rack for 45 minutes. Let sit for 10 minutes before serving. This is delicious served with a spicy salsa on the side (see page 180).

Berry Oatmeal Coffee Cake – serves 10

1 cup light brown sugar

1 teaspoon cinnamon

1 12-ounce tube buttermilk biscuits

1 cup butter, melted

2 cups quick-cooking rolled oats, divided

3 cups fresh or frozen blueberries, raspberries, or blackberries

1 cup sugar

Preheat oven to 375°F. Lightly butter two 9" pie pans. Combine sugar and cinnamon in bowl. Separate dough, cutting each biscuit into quarters. Dip each piece in melted butter, then roll to coat in sugar-cinnamon mixture. Arrange in single layer in pans, and sprinkle each pan with ½ cup rolled oats. Combine berries and remaining sugar mixture. Toss to coat well. Spoon fruit over biscuits, then sprinkle with remaining oats. Drizzle with remaining butter. Bake 20 minutes or until golden brown and center is cooked.

Cut into wedges and serve warm, accompanied by a variety of melon balls, berries, and citrus slices.

Red Chile Cheese Enchiladas – serves 10

Red Chile Sauce
(see page 187)

Guacamole
(see page 187)

Cheese Enchiladas

6 tablespoons vegetable oil

2 dozen blue or yellow corn tortillas

32 ounces grated sharp cheddar cheese

1 head iceberg lettuce, coarsely chopped

5 tomatoes, seeded and coarsely chopped

Preheat oven to 400°F. Heat vegetable oil in medium skillet over medium-high heat. Cook tortillas, one at a time, in oil until slightly crisp—do not overcook. Remove from oil and layer in paper towels until ready to use. Place one tortilla on each plate. Ladle red chile sauce over tortilla to cover. Sprinkle with cheese, and add another tortilla, more sauce, and top with cheese. Place plates in oven until cheese melts and begins to bubble. Carefully remove plates from oven. Garnish with lettuce and top with tomatoes.

Put a dollop of sour cream and guacamole next to the tomatoes, and add a large spoonful of warm black beans to each plate before serving.

Piñon Nut Pie – makes two 9-inch pies, serves 10

Pie Crust
(see page 201)

Filling

8 tablespoons unsalted butter, room temperature

2 cups golden brown sugar

6 eggs

2 cups heavy cream

1 teaspoon salt

3 teaspoons vanilla

2½ cups plus 6 tablespoons piñons

Preheat oven to 400°F. Cream butter and sugar together until light and fluffy. Add eggs, one at a time, and mix well. Add cream, salt, vanilla, and 2½ cups piñons. Pour mixture into unbaked pie crusts and sprinkle with remaining piñons. Bake 15 minutes, reduce heat to 325°F, and continue to bake another 25 minutes.

Let cool completely and serve with a dollop of cinnamon-flavored whipped cream.

Thursday – Day Five
Breakfast

Oven Apple Pancakes

Turkey Sausage

Melon Slices with Lime

Oven Apple Pancakes – serves 10

2 cups milk

6 large eggs, room temperature

1½ cups flour

6 tablespoons sugar

4 cups Granny Smith apples, peeled, cored, and cut into thin slices

3 teaspoons cinnamon

2 teaspoons vanilla

4 tablespoons butter

grated zest from 1 large lemon

powdered sugar and lemon wedges

Preheat oven to 375°F. Whisk milk, eggs, flour, and 4 tablespoons sugar together. Set aside. Mix apples, remaining 2 tablespoons sugar, cinnamon, and vanilla in large bowl. Divide and melt butter in two 9" or 10" oven-proof skillets. Add apple mixture and cook over medium heat until apples are tender. Remove from heat, sprinkle with lemon zest, and pour half of batter over apples in each skillet. Immediately place in oven and bake 30–35 minutes or until golden brown. Remove from oven and cut into wedges.

Serve pancakes with a dusting of powdered sugar and a lemon wedge on the side. Perfect with your favorite turkey sausage and melon slices garnished with lime.

Lunch

Greek-Style Bulgur Salad with Chicken

Crème Caramel Loaf

Greek-Style Bulgur Salad with Chicken – serves 10

4½ cups water

3 cups medium bulgur, uncooked

¾ cup fresh lemon juice, divided

2 teaspoons salt

2½ cups cooked, diced chicken breast

2½ cups cucumber, peeled and chopped

2 cups grape tomatoes, cut in half

1 cup parsley, chopped

½ cup basil leaves, thinly sliced

½ cup red onion, finely diced

½ cup feta cheese, crumbled

¼ cup extra-virgin olive oil

½ teaspoon freshly ground black pepper

10 kalamata olives, pitted and coarsely chopped

Combine water, bulgur, ½ cup lemon juice, and 1 teaspoon salt in medium-size sauce pan and bring to a boil over medium heat. Cover, reduce heat to simmer and cook for 5 minutes. Leaving cover on, remove from heat and let sit, undisturbed, for 15 minutes or until water is absorbed. Uncover and cool to room temperature. Combine remaining ¼ cup lemon juice, remaining 1 teaspoon salt, and remaining ten ingredients in large bowl. Gently toss to mix well. Add cooled bulgur, toss well again to combine. Cover and chill.

Serve over bed of baby greens.

Crème Caramel Loaf – serves 8

(I usually double this and use two loaf pans
to ensure I have enough for seconds!)

1 cup sugar

1 tablespoon water

1½ cups milk

½ cup heavy cream

4 large eggs

4 large egg yolks

Preheat oven to 325°F. In a medium skillet, combine ½ cup sugar
with the water and cook over high heat until deep amber, about
4 minutes, swirling the pan occasionally. Immediately pour the
caramel into an 8 x 4½ x 3" metal loaf pan, turning to evenly
coat the bottom. Let the caramel harden. In a bowl, whisk
remaining ½ cup sugar, milk, cream, eggs, and egg yolks. Pour
the custard into the prepared pan, set in a small baking dish, and
add enough water to the dish to reach halfway up the side of the
pan. Bake for 50 minutes or until set around the edges but still
slightly soft in the center. Remove the pan from the water bath
and let cool to room temperature. Refrigerate until chilled, at
least 4 hours.* Run a thin knife around the edge of the custard.
Invert a rectangular plate or platter over the pan and flip, tapping
to loosen and unmold the custard. Spoon any remaining caramel
from the pan onto the custard loaf. Cut into slices and serve.

* This can be refrigerated overnight before unmolding.

Dinner

Roasted Beef Tenderloin

Roasted Root Vegetables

Baby Romaine Salad with Garlic Croutons

and Sherry Shallot Dressing

Lemon Cake with Pineapple, Anise, and Rum Sauce

Roasted Beef Tenderloin – serves 8–10

5 pounds beef tenderloin, trimmed

coarse salt and fresh pepper

olive oil for searing

Preheat oven to 400°F. Season the roast with salt and pepper. Heat olive oil in large sauté pan until it begins to smoke. Turn on exhaust fan, add the beef, and sear well on all sides, including both tips. Transfer beef to rack in a shallow roasting pan and cook until medium rare (120°F internal temperature or about 20 minutes). Remove from oven, loosely wrap in foil, and let rest 10 minutes before carving.

Roasted Root Vegetables – serves 6–8

1 bunch beets (about 1½ pounds), trimmed but not peeled, cut into ½-inch pieces

1 head of garlic, cloves separated and peeled

2 tablespoons olive oil

salt and freshly ground pepper

2½ pounds butternut squash, peeled, seeded, cut into ½-inch pieces

1 large turnip, peeled, cut into ½-inch pieces

1½ pounds Yukon Gold potatoes, unpeeled, cut into ½-inch pieces

1 medium red onion, cut into ½-inch pieces

Preheat oven to 425°F. Oil large, rimmed baking sheets. Place beets and one half of the garlic cloves on one baking sheet. Drizzle with olive oil and salt and fresh pepper. Toss to coat. Combine squash, turnip, potatoes, onion, and remaining garlic cloves in very large bowl. Toss to coat. Divide vegetables between prepared baking sheets and spread evenly. Sprinkle generously with salt and pepper. Roast vegetables until tender and golden brown, stirring occasionally, about 1 hour. Carefully watch the beets because they can burn quite easily.

Divide the vegetable mixture among the plates, beginning with the squash-potato mixture and topping with the beets.

Baby Romaine Salad with Garlic Croutons and Sherry Shallot Dressing – serves 10

5 tablespoons extra-virgin olive oil

4 garlic cloves, pressed

8 slices sourdough bread

3 tablespoons sea salt

2 teaspoons pepper

32 ounces baby romaine leaves

30 cherry tomatoes, cut in half

Garlic Croutons

Preheat oven to 350°F. Pour the olive oil in small bowl and mix with pressed garlic. Set aside. Remove the crust from bread slices and cut or tear into 1-inch cubes. Place in large mixing bowl. Pour in oil-garlic mixture and toss to coat the bread cubes. Sprinkle salt and pepper over the bread and toss again. Pour the croutons onto a rimmed baking sheet and bake for 20 minutes or until the croutons begin to turn brown. Remove from oven and let cool.

Divide the lettuce between the plates, and add the tomatoes and croutons. Serve the dressing on the side.

Sherry Shallot Vinaigrette
(see page 190)

Lemon Cake with Pineapple, Anise, and Rum Sauce – serves 10–12

Lemon Cake

butter and fine bread crumbs to prepare the cooking pan

3 cups sifted flour

2 teaspoons baking powder

$\frac{1}{2}$ teaspoon salt

8 ounces unsalted butter (2 sticks)

2 cups sugar

4 large eggs, room temperature

1 cup buttermilk

zest of 2 lemons, finely grated

Preheat oven to 350°F and move rack to lower half of oven. Butter pan and lightly dust with fine bread crumbs. Set aside. Sift together flour, baking powder, and salt. Set aside. In large mixing bowl, beat the butter until soft with an electric beater. Add sugar and beat until mixture is light and fluffy. Beat in eggs one at a time, scraping the bowl as necessary with a rubber spatula. Using the lowest speed, alternately add the dry ingredients and the buttermilk into the sugar-egg mixture until just mixed. Fold in the lemon zest. Pour this thick batter into the prepared pan and bake approximately 1 hour or until a cake tester (toothpick is my tool of choice) comes out clean. Remove from the oven and let sit for 5 minutes. Then invert over a cooking rack and remove from pan. Let cool completely before serving.

Place cake wedges on individual plates, and spoon on a generous portion of the rum sauce, making sure to include the fruit. A dollop of whipped cream is a nice touch.

Pineapple, Anise, and Rum Sauce –
makes about $1\frac{1}{2}$ cups

2 cups sugar

2 cups water

2 vanilla beans, split lengthwise

6 star anise or 3 tablespoons anise seed, lightly toasted

2 fresh pineapples, peeled, cored, and cut into quarters

6 tablespoons high-grade, light Puerto Rican rum

Over medium-high heat, combine sugar with 2 cups water in medium sauce pan. Stir until sugar dissolves. Reduce heat and simmer for 15 minutes. Remove from heat. Immediately add vanilla beans and anise. Let cool completely. Cut pineapple into bite-size pieces and add to the syrup. Add rum. Stir gently to mix together. Chill for 2 hours or up to 3 days, covered in refrigerator.

Friday – Day Six
(Farewell)
Continental Breakfast

English Muffins, Bagels,

Cream Cheese, Fruit Jam,

Orange Juice, Fresh Melon Slices,

Yogurt, Granola, and Coffee and Tea

To see a hillside white with dogwood bloom is to know

a particular ecstasy of beauty, but to walk the gray Winter woods

and find the buds which will resurrect that beauty in another

May is to partake of continuity.

— Hal Borland

Spring

*The air and the earth interpenetrated in the warm
gusts of spring; the soil was full of sunlight,
and the sunlight full of red dust. The air one breathed
was saturated with earthy smells, and the grass under
foot had a reflection of the blue sky in it.*

— Willa Cather

As the weather begins to warm, thoughts in Santa Fe are turning
to spring. Santa Fe is the nation's oldest capital, founded in 1610,
the nation's highest capital, at 7,000 feet, and it claims the
nation's oldest church, San Miguel Chapel, as well as the oldest
public building, the Palace of the Governors, now a museum.
This is a city with not only a lengthy history but also memorable
charm and grace. Spring literally blasts its way into town, with
fierce winds buffeting everything in their paths and leaving newly
sprouted, bright green aspen leaves quivering and dancing. The
months of March, April, and May can be rainy, cloudy, or
sunny—and are often heartbreakingly beautiful as daffodils
bloom, robins poke for worms in wet lawns, red-winged blackbirds
take to the air, and birdsong trills as nest building begins.

Spring is an ideal time to visit the Rio Grande. Its name alone
evokes romantic images of old John Wayne westerns—and the
river has played a real-life, dramatic role in shaping the history

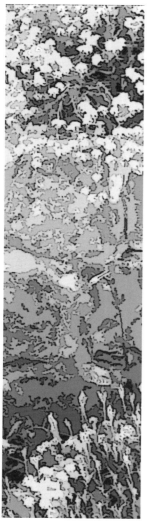

of this part of the Southwest as generations of Native American, Hispanic, and Anglo farmers and settlers have organized their lives around its life-giving flow. Spring floods signal the beginning of planting season. Both older and newer pueblos and farming communities stand along the banks where the river runs wild between the Colorado/New Mexico border down past Taos, rages through a narrow gorge edged with sage and boulders, and heads through New Mexico's heartland into Texas.

Santa Fe Plaza, in the center of the downtown area, abounds with shops, restaurants, galleries, museums, cafes, and historic sites radiating in every direction. Strolling along Canyon Road reveals an eclectic mix of Spanish-Pueblo, Spanish colonial, and American territorial architecture, representing the numerous and frequent changes this road has undergone over the years. Today, it's the heart of Santa Fe's art scene. Scores of galleries line each side, featuring paintings, drawings, sculptures, hand-woven textiles, pottery, mixed media, photography, and antiques.

Santa Fe is that unique and special combination of both the best of cultural attractions and breathtaking opportunities for enjoying natural beauty and wildlife, all within or just outside the town. As a setting for those who come to the School for Advanced Research to think, to write, to further the scope of their research, it is at once embracing and inspiring.

WELCOME DINNER
Saturday

Spaghetti with Fresh Tomato and Basil Sauce

Baby Greens Salad with Italian Vinaigrette

Angel Food Cake with Strawberries

Italian Vinaigrette –

makes 2 cups

½ cup red wine vinegar

1 teaspoon sea salt

1½ cups extra-virgin olive oil

freshly ground black pepper to taste

Whisk the vinegar and salt together until the salt dissolves. Slowly whisk in the oil until the dressing is well blended.

Serve over a bed of baby greens.

Spaghetti with Fresh Tomato and Basil Sauce – serves 10

6 pounds Roma tomatoes, halved lengthwise, then cut into sixths

20 basil leaves

4 cloves garlic, thinly sliced

2 16-ounce packages spaghetti

fresh parmesan cheese, shredded

Cut tomatoes and place in large, heavy-duty pot with lid. Bring to boil and immediately reduce heat to simmer. Add 10 basil leaves and garlic. Simmer 5 hours, stirring occasionally. Adjust heat to avoid scorching on the bottom of the pot. After 5 hours, coarsely mash mixture with a potato masher, and remove lid to allow sauce to thicken. Add remaining basil leaves and cook 1 additional hour. Cook spaghetti according to directions, drain, and rinse twice with warm water. Dump cooked pasta back into pot and lightly toss with one cup of sauce.

Put spaghetti in individual pasta bowls, and ladle enough sauce over it to cover the pasta. Have plenty of fresh, shredded parmesan cheese available on the table.

Angel Food Cake with Strawberries – serves 10–12

I use a packaged mix for my angel food cakes. The altitude (see page viii) wreaks havoc on this type of cake, and it has been very hard for me to come up with a consistent recipe.

Strawberries

1 pound of fresh strawberries, cleaned, stemmed, and cut into quarters. Sprinkle with ½ cup powdered sugar and set aside until ready to use.

Spoon strawberries and a bit of the juice over each slice of cake. You may want to serve this with a small dollop of whipped cream, but that will certainly increase the calorie count!

Sunday – Day One
Breakfast

Scrambled Eggs with Green Chile and Cheese

Mango and Grape Salad

Scrambled Eggs with Green Chile and Cheese – serves 10

20 large eggs

4 tablespoons water

1 teaspoon salt

1 teaspoon freshly ground pepper

2 tablespoons butter

2 cups chopped green chiles

½ pound sharp cheddar cheese, finely grated

Break the eggs into a large bowl, add water, salt, and pepper and whisk until eggs are well blended. Do not over-whisk, as it will make the eggs tough. Preheat large skillet, and melt butter over medium-high heat.* As soon as butter is melted, pour in egg mixture and gently stir as the eggs begin to set. Add green chile and cook for another 2 minutes; then add cheese. Continue to stir eggs gently until cheese is melted and the eggs are completely set. Serve immediately. Slices of maple-cured bacon complement this dish nicely.

* You may have to use two skillets if one is not large enough, or cook eggs in two separate batches. If you cook the eggs in two batches, remove the first batch from the skillet and place in a large bowl. Loosely cover, allowing some of the steam to be released. Serve as soon as possible.

Mango and Grape Salad – serves 10

7 ripe mangoes

1 pound green or red seedless grapes

juice of 1½ limes

1 tablespoon powdered sugar

10 mint leaves

Slice and peel mangoes, cutting into bite-size pieces. Place in medium-size bowl. Wash grapes and cut in half. Place in bowl with mango pieces. Mix lime juice and powdered sugar in small bowl. Pour over mango and grapes. Cover and refrigerate for 30 minutes. Garnish with mint leaves and serve.

Lunch

Rustic Spring Vegetable Stew
(Chile) Cheese Cornbread
Strawberry Misu

(Chile) Cheese Cornbread –

serves 9

1 cup cornmeal (or if using blue corn, ½ cup blue meal and ½ cup white flour)

1 cup creamed corn

¾ cup milk

⅓ cup vegetable oil

2 eggs, slightly beaten

½ teaspoon baking soda

1 teaspoon salt

1½ cups grated cheddar cheese

1 cup chopped green chiles (optional)

Preheat oven to 350°F. Mix together cornmeal, corn, milk, oil, eggs, baking soda, and salt. Fold in 1½ cups grated cheddar cheese and, if desired, 1 cup chopped green chiles. Bake for 40 minutes in a buttered 8 x 8" square baking dish or a 9" round skillet at least 2" deep.

Rustic Spring Vegetable Stew – serves 8

6 cups frozen artichoke hearts

⅓ cup lemon juice

2 onions

2 heads fresh fennel

1 head romaine lettuce

¼ cup olive oil

5 cups water

2 cups frozen peas

salt and pepper

freshly ground pecorino romano or parmesan cheese

Thaw and drain artichokes. Place in bowl with lemon juice. Peel onions, cut in half, then slice lengthwise into ¼-inch-thick slivers. Rinse fennel; trim off and discard stalks and root ends (reserve a few leafy sprigs for garnish, if desired). Cut heads lengthwise into about ¼-inch matchsticks. Rinse lettuce well, and trim off and discard core. Cut leaves into 3-inch lengths. Drain lemon juice off artichokes. In a 5–6 quart pan over medium-high heat, frequently stir artichokes, onions, and fennel in olive oil until onions are limp. Add water and bring to a boil over high heat. Cover, reduce heat, and simmer, stirring occasionally until artichokes are tender, about 6 minutes. Add peas, bring mixture to a boil over high heat, and cook until peas are tender, about 2–3 minutes. Stir in lettuce and cook until barely wilted, about 30 seconds. Add salt and pepper to taste.

Ladle stew into bowls and garnish with reserved fennel sprigs. Sprinkle with cheese to taste.

Strawberry Misu– serves 8

1¼ cups strawberry preserves

⅓ cup, plus 4 tablespoons kept separate, orange liqueur

⅓ cup fresh orange or blood orange juice

1 pound mascarpone cheese, room temperature

1½ cups whipping cream

⅓ cup sugar

1 teaspoon vanilla extract

1½ pounds fresh strawberries

52 ladyfinger cookies

Whisk preserves, ⅓ cup orange liqueur, and juice in a small bowl (2-cup size works best). Set aside. Pour 2 of the remaining tablespoons of orange liqueur into a large bowl. Fold in mascarpone until just blended. Using electric mixer, beat cream, sugar, vanilla, and remaining 2 tablespoons of orange liqueur together in large bowl. Beat to soft peaks. Stir a quarter of the whipped cream mixture into the mascarpone mixture. Fold remaining whipped cream into the mascarpone. Core and slice half of the strawberries and set aside. Spread ½ cup preserve mixture over bottom of 12 x 9 x 2" glass baking dish. Cover with ladyfingers. Spoon ¾ cup preserve mixture over ladyfingers; then spread 2½ cups mascarpone mixture over the top. Arrange sliced berries over mascarpone mixture. Repeat layering with remaining ladyfingers, preserves, and mascarpone. Cover and chill at least 8 hours or overnight.

Slice remaining strawberries, arrange over top of dessert, and serve.

Dinner

Mama G's Hafa Da Chicken

Fried Potatoes and Onions

Arugula and Baby Spinach Salad with Citrus Dressing

Vanilla Sour Cream Panna Cotta with Berry Wine Compote

Mama G's Hafa Da Chicken – serves 6–8

1 onion, chopped

1 cup soy sauce

1 cup fresh lemon juice

1½ cups sugar

2 chickens, cut and skinned

garlic salt

lemon pepper

Coarsely chop onion and place in medium-size bowl. Add soy sauce, lemon juice, and sugar. Stir to blend; taste (should taste like a teriyaki marinade, so add more of any of the three main ingredients to create the taste you like). Skin the chicken, and generously sprinkle each piece with the garlic salt and lemon pepper. Place in large baggie. Pour marinade over chicken and marinate in refrigerator for 6–24 hours. Let sit at room temperature at least 3 hours before cooking. Remove chicken from bags and place on platter. Reserve marinade. Cook chicken over medium-heat grill for 25 minutes, turning every 5–8 minutes and basting with marinade each time. Remove from grill and cover with tin foil until ready to serve.*

*This chicken can be served hot or cold and is excellent the second day. Leftovers make a terrific chicken salad when mixed with mango, walnuts, celery, and a very light oriental dressing.

Fried Potatoes and Onions – serves 10

12 russet potatoes, scrubbed and peeled

2 medium yellow onions

8 teaspoons butter (1 stick)

salt and pepper to taste

Using a food processor with the slicing blade, thinly slice potatoes and place in large bowl of cold, salted water. Set aside until ready to use. Peel onions and cut in half (top to bottom). Thinly slice. Melt butter in large skillet over medium-high heat. Add onions and cook until well coated with the butter and beginning to soften. Drain the potatoes and add to the skillet, stirring well to mix with the onions. Continue to cook for 30 minutes, turning occasionally, until potatoes are tender. The potatoes should have crisp, brown edges, and the onions should be golden. Sprinkle with salt and pepper. Remove skillet from heat and serve immediately.

Citrus Dressing – makes 2 cups

½ cup freshly squeezed orange juice (1 large orange)

½ cup freshly squeezed lemon juice (2 large lemons)

1 teaspoon salt

1¾ cups extra-virgin olive oil

freshly ground pepper

Whisk the orange and lemon juices together with the salt until the salt dissolves. Slowly whisk in olive oil until well blended. Season with pepper to taste.

Serve over a bed of arugula and baby spinach.

Vanilla Sour Cream Panna Cotta – serves 8

2½ teaspoons unflavored gelatin

¼ cup water

1¼ cups evaporated fat-free milk

½ cup powdered sugar

2 vanilla beans, split lengthwise

2 cups sour cream

¼ cup ground cardamom

Sprinkle gelatin over water in small bowl and let stand 10 minutes. Mix milk, powdered sugar, and vanilla beans in medium saucepan and bring to boil over medium-high heat. Remove from heat and remove vanilla beans. Scrape vanilla seeds from the beans and add back into the milk mixture. Discard the beans. Add gelatin mixture to milk mixture and whisk until gelatin dissolves. Add sour cream and cardamom and stir until well blended. Divide mixture evenly between eight 6-ounce ramekins or custard cups. Cover and refrigerate at least 8 hours. To serve, loosen edges of custard with a knife or rubber spatula. Place a dessert plate upside down over the top of the ramekin and flip over. The custard should easily fall out onto the plate.

Serve with berry compote and sprig of mint.

Berry Wine Compote –
makes approximately 2 cups

3 cups frozen berries, thawed and divided

¼ cup fruity, dry wine

3 tablespoons sugar

mint sprigs, for garnish

Place 1 cup berries, the wine, and the sugar into a food processor and mix until smooth. If using seeded berries such as black or raspberries, strain the mixture through a fine sieve before pouring into a sauce pan. Heat mixture to a boil over medium-high heat and cook for 1 minute. Remove from heat and fold in remaining 2 cups berries.

Cool completely before serving. Add mint garnish.

Monday – Day Two
Breakfast

Blue Corn Waffles with Piñons

Turkey Sausage

Melon Balls with Mint-Citrus Dressing

Blue Corn Waffles with Piñons – serves 10

1 cup flour

1 cup blue cornmeal

4 teaspoons baking powder

1 teaspoon salt

½ cup vegetable oil

2 eggs

whole milk

2 cups roasted piñons

Mix flour, cornmeal, baking powder, and salt in large mixing bowl. Add vegetable oil and eggs. Slowly add milk, whisking constantly, until you reach the desired consistency. Heat waffle iron; when it is hot, oil lightly. Pour in one ladle of batter (or amount suggested by manufacturer of waffle maker) and cook until done.*

Place waffles on warmed plates and sprinkle with piñons. Serve with warm maple syrup and turkey sausage on the side.

*May be kept in 200°F oven on oven racks (not on cookie sheets) until ready to serve.

Melon Balls with Mint-Citrus Dressing – serves 10

1 cantaloupe

1 honeydew melon

½ small watermelon

½ cup orange juice

¼ cup lime juice

2 tablespoons fresh lemon juice

lemon zest from 2 lemons, grated

10 fresh mint leaves, slivered

Using a melon baller, carve out the melons, placing the balls and remaining juice from the melons in a large bowl. If you do not have a melon baller, you may cut the fruit into bite-size pieces. Combine juices together in a food processor. Transfer to bowl and fold in lemon zest and mint. Cover and refrigerate at least 1 hour and up to 4 hours. Gently stir to re-blend before pouring over melon balls.

Lunch

Sofrito-Style Red Beans and Rice

Baby Romaine Salad with Pears

Fruit Sorbet with Oatmeal-Raisin Cookies

Sofrito-Style Red Beans and Rice – serves 10

8 bacon slices

1 teaspoon olive oil

1½ cups onion, chopped

½ cup green bell pepper, chopped

½ cup red bell pepper, chopped

5 garlic cloves, minced

2 tablespoons tomato paste

2 cups uncooked long-grain rice

1½ teaspoons dried oregano

1½ teaspoons ground cumin

1 teaspoon salt

1 teaspoon freshly ground pepper

1 bay leaf

2 cups water

5½ cups chicken broth

6 cups canned red beans, rinsed and drained

5 thinly sliced scallions for garnish

Cook bacon in heavy stock pot until crisp. Remove bacon and crumble. Pour off all but 1 tablespoon of bacon drippings. Add oil, onion, and bell peppers to remaining bacon drippings in pot and sauté until onion is tender, about 4 minutes. Add garlic and sauté until garlic begins to turn brown. Add tomato paste and cook another minute, stirring constantly. Add rice, oregano, cumin, salt, and pepper. Cook for 2 minutes, stirring to coat rice. Put crumbled bacon back into pot with bay leaf, water, and 3 cups chicken broth. Bring to a boil, cover, and simmer for 25 minutes or until rice is tender. Remove from heat, remove bay leaf, and stir in beans and remaining 2½ cups chicken broth. Cook another 5 minutes over low heat or until heated through, occasionally stirring.

Garnish with sliced scallions. Place several containers of hot sauce on the table for those who like things a bit spicier.

Baby Romaine Salad with Pears
– serves 10

2 14-ounce packages baby romaine greens

5 red pears, cored and sliced

2 tablespoons fresh lemon juice

Distribute the greens evenly among 10 plates. Core the pears; then cut each one into 10 slivers, and place 5 slivers in a fan shape on each salad. Sprinkle lemon juice on the pears to keep them from turning brown. Serve immediately.

Fruit Sorbet with Oatmeal-Raisin Cookies

Oatmeal-Raisin Cookies – makes 4½ dozen

1½ cups quick-cook rolled oats

¾ cup flour

½ teaspoon cinnamon

½ teaspoon baking soda

8 tablespoons unsalted butter, room temperature

½ cup brown sugar, packed

½ cup sugar

1 egg

1 tablespoon vanilla

½ cup raisins, coarsely chopped

¼ cup walnuts, coarsely chopped

Mix oats, flour, cinnamon, and baking soda together in a bowl. With an electric mixer, cream the butter and sugars together in a large bowl until light and fluffy. Beat in the egg and vanilla. Slowly beat in the dry ingredients, adding the raisins and walnuts last. Cover large bowl of cookie dough and put in refrigerator for at least 1 hour.

When ready to bake, preheat oven to 350°F, and lightly grease cookie sheets. Using rounded teaspoonfuls, drop the batter onto the prepared baking sheets, spacing the mounds 2 inches apart. Bake until golden, approximately 10 minutes. Leave the cookies on the baking sheets for 2 minutes, then transfer to wire racks to cool. Store in airtight container.

To accompany the cookies, I like to use a combination of raspberry and lemon fruit sorbets. Putting a scoop of each in a medium-size ramekin makes the dish beautiful, as well as mighty tasty.

Dinner

Fish Tacos with Fresh Pineapple Salsa

New Mexico–Style Spanish Rice

Mexican Cole Slaw

Chocolate Custard

Fresh Pineapple Salsa –
makes
approximately
3 cups

1 large pineapple,
peeled, cored, and
cut into small,
bite-size pieces

1½ jalapeños, finely
diced

1 red bell pepper,
finely diced

3 tablespoons rice
wine vinegar

juice of 1 lime

Prepare pineapple
and place in medium-
size glass, ceramic,
or plastic bowl. Add
diced jalapeños and
red bell pepper to
pineapple; then pour
vinegar and lime
juice over all. Toss
to mix well. Cover
and refrigerate.

Let sit at room tem-
perature for 1 hour
before serving.

Fish Tacos with Fresh Pineapple Salsa –
serves 10

Fish Tacos

2 eggs, slightly beaten

3 cups bread crumbs

1 tablespoon sea salt

1 tablespoon freshly ground black pepper

1 tablespoon red chile powder

¼ cup extra-virgin olive oil

20 Tilapia fillets

20 corn tortillas

cilantro sprigs, for garnish

lemon slices

Break eggs into shallow baking dish and gently beat. Pour bread crumbs into a second shallow baking dish. Add salt, pepper, and chile powder and stir to mix well. Heat oil in heavy-duty skillet over medium-high heat until simmering. In small batches, dip fish fillets in egg mixture, then roll in bread crumbs. Carefully place breaded fillet in skillet and cook 5 minutes or until browned. Turn over and cook additional 3 minutes. Remove from skillet and place on platter. Cover loosely with tinfoil and continue cooking until all fillets are done. Loosely wrap tortillas in plastic wrap or in a clean, slightly dampened tea towel and heat in microwave for 30–40 seconds.

Place two warmed tortillas on each plate, and position one fish fillet on each tortilla. Garnish with cilantro sprig and several lemon wedges. Serve immediately with pineapple salsa on the side.

New Mexico–Style Spanish Rice – serves 10

1 medium onion, cut into quarters

6 Roma tomatoes, cut into quarters, or 1 14-ounce can oven-roasted tomatoes

1 tablespoon salt

4 tablespoons olive oil

3 cups basmati rice

6 garlic cloves

4 fresh sage leaves

2 bay leaves

1 teaspoon cumin seeds

1 teaspoon black mustard seeds

1 tablespoon plus 2 teaspoons sea salt

6 cups vegetable broth or stock

Preheat oven to 375°F. Place onion and tomato slices on lightly greased, rimmed baking sheet. Sprinkle with salt and roast for 20 minutes. Remove from oven. When cool enough to handle, remove skins from the tomatoes. Cut tomatoes and onion into ½-inch chunks and set aside. Heat oil in large skillet. Add rice and cook, stirring until the rice is golden, about 4–5 minutes. Stir in the tomatoes, onion, and all remaining ingredients and bring to a simmer. Spoon rice mixture into lightly greased casserole with tight-fitting lid and bake at 375°F for 30 minutes or until all the liquid has been absorbed and the rice is tender. Remove from oven and let sit for 10 minutes undisturbed before serving.

Mexican Cole Slaw – serves 6

1 head cabbage, finely chopped

juice of ½–1 lime (use sparingly)

1½ teaspoons cumin

Pour lime juice over chopped cabbage. Sprinkle with cumin and toss to coat well. Serve immediately.

Chocolate Custard – serves 10

1¼ cups whole milk

15 tablespoons sugar

5 large egg yolks

15 ounces bittersweet chocolate, finely chopped

1 teaspoon Mexican cinnamon, ground

¼ teaspoon salt

10 tablespoons unsalted butter, softened

2½ cups whipping cream

Combine the milk and 10 tablespoons of the sugar in sauce pan and heat until steaming and the sugar is dissolved. Break egg yolks in small bowl, and gradually whisk in the hot milk. Return mixture to the saucepan and cook over medium heat, whisking constantly, until slightly thickened, about 4 minutes. Remove from heat and add the chocolate, cinnamon, and salt, whisking until smooth. Whisk in butter. Pour into shallow custard bowls and refrigerate briefly, at least 5 minutes.* Beat whipping cream, adding remaining 5 tablespoons of sugar until soft peaks appear. Dollop cream on top of custard and top with dash of cinnamon and chocolate shavings.

* May be made to this point in advance and chilled overnight, then served slightly chilled or at room temperature.

Tuesday – Day Three
Continental Breakfast

English Muffins, Bagels,
Cream Cheese, Fruit Jam,
Orange Juice, Fresh Melon Slices,
Yogurt, Granola, and Coffee and Tea

Lunch

Tomato-Peanut Soup with Couscous and Tomato Croutons
Mixed Greens Salad with Champagne Vinaigrette
Coconut Cupcakes with Cream Cheese Icing

Tomato-Peanut Soup with Couscous and Tomato Croutons – serves 8

Tomato Croutons

20 cherry tomatoes, halved

1 cup olive oil

2 teaspoons sugar

salt

sourdough bread, cut into ½–inch cubes

Preheat oven to 250°F. Place cherry tomato halves on baking tray, cut side up. Sprinkle with olive oil, sugar, and salt. Arrange bread cubes around tomatoes and bake 45 minutes or until bread is toasted and tomatoes begin to shrivel. Set aside.

Tomato-Peanut Soup

4 28-ounce cans diced tomatoes, drained (reserve juice) (Fire-roasted are the tastiest!)

12 garlic cloves, minced

2 habanero chiles, chopped (try one the first time you make it—they are very, very hot)

6 shallots, minced

2 quarts vegetable broth

2 cups couscous, prepared

12 arugula leaves, shredded, for garnish

4 basil leaves, shredded, for garnish

Preheat oven to 425°F. Combine tomatoes, garlic, chiles, and shallots in roasting pan. Roast 45 minutes, stirring occasionally. Transfer to large stockpot and add vegetable broth and reserved tomato juice. Bring to a boil, reduce heat to low, and simmer 20 minutes. Purée in food processor in small batches until smooth.* Return to pot and keep warm until serving.

Garnish with 1½ cups of couscous, a few cherry tomatoes from the crouton recipe, and some of the croutons. Then sprinkle with arugula and basil slivers.

*To spice this up, add 1 cup peanut butter to soup mix at the time you are using the processor.

Coconut Cupcakes – makes 18–20 large

¾ pound unsalted butter, room temperature

2 cups sugar

5 extra-large eggs, room temperature

1½ teaspoons vanilla extract

1½ teaspoons almond extract

3 cups flour

1 teaspoon baking powder

½ teaspoon baking soda

½ teaspoon salt

1 cup buttermilk

14 ounces sweetened, shredded coconut

Preheat oven to 325°F. Cream butter and sugar until light and fluffy, about 5 minutes. Add the eggs one at a time, using low speed, scraping down the bowl after each addition. Add the vanilla and almond extracts and mix well. In separate bowl, sift together the flour, baking powder, baking soda, and salt. In three parts, alternately add the dry ingredients and the buttermilk to the batter, beginning and ending with the dry. Mix until just combined. Fold in 7 ounces of coconut. Line muffin pan with paper liners. Fill each cup to the top with batter (an ice cream scoop works well!). Bake for 25–35 minutes, until the tops are brown and a toothpick comes out clean. Allow to cool in the pan for 15 minutes. Remove to a baking rack and cool completely. Frost with cream cheese icing and sprinkle with the remaining coconut.

Cream Cheese Icing

1 pound cream cheese, room temperature

¾ pound unsalted butter, room temperature

1 teaspoon vanilla extract

½ teaspoon almond extract

1½ pounds confectioners' sugar, sifted

Blend together the cream cheese, butter, and both extracts. Add the sugar and mix until smooth.

Champagne Vinaigrette –
makes 2 cups

½ cup champagne vinegar

1 teaspoon sea salt

1½ cups extra-virgin olive oil

freshly ground black pepper to taste

Whisk the vinegar and salt together until the salt dissolves. Slowly whisk in the oil until the dressing is well blended. Season with pepper.

Serve over a bed of mixed greens.

Dinner

*On Tuesdays, the custom is for
the president of the School to take
the seminar participants out to dinner
at one of Santa Fe's many fine restaurants.
The brisk mountain spring whips up the appetite,
and the season's fresh vegetables are just making
their first appearance on local menus.*

Wednesday – Day Four
Breakfast

*Breakfast Burritos with Bacon and Cheese
Red and Green Chile
Strawberry Salsa*

Breakfast Burritos with Bacon and Cheese – serves 10

20 slices bacon

20 large eggs

salt and pepper

16 ounces sharp cheddar cheese, finely grated

10 large flour tortillas, wrapped in damp paper towel
    and heated in microwave for 1 minute

Fry bacon in large, heavy-duty skillet until golden brown and crisp. Remove from skillet and set aside. Break eggs into mixing bowl and whisk until well blended. Add salt and pepper. Pour eggs into preheated skillet, scrambling just until eggs are set but not dry. Mix in 10 ounces of cheese. Spoon about ½ cup of egg mixture in the center of a warm tortilla, leaving 1-inch space at both the top and bottom of the tortilla. Lay 2 pieces of bacon over the egg mixture, and quickly fold bottom of tortilla up to cover lower portion of egg mixture. Fold over both sides of tortilla and place on warmed plate, with folded edges on bottom. Spoon several tablespoons of red or green chile over top of burrito and sprinkle with additional cheese. Serve immediately.

Red Chile Sauce
(see page 187)

Green Chile Sauce
(see page 18)

Heat chile in covered sauce pan until warm—do not boil!

Strawberry Salsa
– serves 10

1½ pounds fresh strawberries, cleaned, stemmed, and coarsely chopped

3 scallions, thinly sliced, using both the white and the green portions

1 ounce cilantro leaves, coarsely chopped

2½ teaspoons fresh lemon juice

½ teaspoon salt

Gently mix all ingredients together. This does taste better when served at room temperature, but if you don't plan to use it immediately, it can be covered and refrigerated for up to 4 hours.

Lunch

Minestrone Soup

Seminar House Blue Corn Madeleines

Peach-Raspberry Slab Pie

Minestrone Soup – serves 6–8

¾ cup (about 2 small) leeks, sliced thin

¾ cup (about 2 medium) carrots, finely diced

¾ cup (about 2 stalks) celery, finely diced

¾ cup (about 2 small) onions, finely diced

1¼ cups (about 1) russet potato, peeled, coarsely diced

1¼ cups (about 1) zucchini, coarsely diced

3 cups spinach leaves, cut into thin strips

1 28-ounce can whole tomatoes, drained and chopped

8 cups water

1 parmesan cheese rind

1 teaspoon salt

1 10-ounce can cannelloni beans, drained and rinsed

¼ cup basil pesto

additional salt and pepper to taste

½ cup dried pasta (optional)*

Bring vegetables, tomatoes, water, cheese rind, and 1 teaspoon salt to boil in large pot. Reduce heat to medium-low and simmer uncovered, stirring occasionally, until vegetables are tender but still hold their shape, about 1 hour. Add beans and cook until heated through, about 5 minutes. Remove pot from heat and discard cheese rind. Stir in pesto. Adjust seasonings with salt and pepper. This soup can be refrigerated in an airtight container for 3 days or frozen for 1 month.

*If adding pasta, add before beans and cook until tender, according to package instructions.

Seminar House Blue Corn Madeleines
– makes about 36 mini-muffins*

1 cup blue cornmeal

1 cup flour

5 tablespoons sugar

1 tablespoon baking powder

$\frac{1}{2}$ teaspoon cardamom

$\frac{1}{4}$ teaspoon cinnamon

$\frac{1}{4}$ teaspoon nutmeg

$\frac{1}{2}$ teaspoon salt

1 cup whole milk

1 large egg, beaten to blend

5 tablespoons unsalted butter, melted

Preheat oven to 350°F. Whisk cornmeal, flour, sugar, baking powder, cardamom, cinnamon, nutmeg, and salt in large bowl to combine. Stir in milk, egg, and butter. Spoon 1 heaping tablespoon into cups of buttered Madeleine mold (or a mini-muffin tin). Bake until golden brown, about 8–11 minutes. Turn out onto cooling rack and cool completely.

*Can be made 1 day ahead. Store in airtight container at room temperature.

Peach-Raspberry Slab Pie – serves 16

2¼ pounds peaches (9), peeled, pitted, and cut into thin wedges

1 cup raspberries (6 ounces)

1 cup sugar

¼ cup cornstarch

1 tablespoon fresh lemon juice

⅛ teaspoon salt

1 large egg yolk

1 tablespoon heavy cream

4 tablespoons sugar for sprinkling

First, prepare in advance TWO batches Pâte Brisée (see sidebar).

Then, preheat oven to 375°F, with rack in lower third. Toss peaches, raspberries, sugar, cornstarch, lemon juice, and salt in large bowl. Transfer half of dough to lightly floured surface and roll into a 12 x 16" rectangle that is ⅛ inch thick. Coat a 15¼ x 10½" rimmed baking sheet with cooking spray. Line baking sheet with parchment paper, leaving a 1-inch overhang on long sides. Transfer dough to prepared baking sheet. Trim edges of dough to hang over sides of baking sheet by ½ inch. Roll out the remaining dough into another 12 x 16" rectangle that is ⅛ inch thick. Pour fruit mixture onto the dough-lined baking sheet. Cover with the remaining layer of dough. Trim edges of dough to hang over sides by ½ inch. Fold edges of top layer over edges of bottom layer and pinch to seal. Cut about 30 holes out of the top of crust, using a ½-inch round pastry tip, spacing evenly. Whisk together egg yolk and cream in small bowl. Brush crust with egg wash and sprinkle with sugar. Bake until crust turns golden and filling is bubbling, about 1 hour and 10 minutes. If crust is browning too quickly, tent pie with foil and continue baking. Let cool completely on wire rack, about 3 hours. Pull up parchment to remove from baking sheet.

Pâte Brisée –
makes ONE
12 x 18" rectangle

2½ cups flour

1½ teaspoons coarse salt

1 teaspoon sugar

2 sticks, cold unsalted butter, cut into small pieces

6–8 tablespoons ice water

Combine flour, salt, and sugar in food processor. Add butter and process until the mixture resembles coarse meal, about 10 seconds. With machine running, add ice water in a slow, steady stream just until dough comes together—not more than 30 seconds! Turn dough onto a piece of plastic wrap. Flatten dough and shape into rectangle. Refrigerate at least 1 hour or overnight or freeze up to a month.

Dinner

Grilled Chile-Marinated Pork Loins with Avocado Salsa

Oven-Roasted Sweet Potatoes

Asparagus with Lemon and Garlic

Carrot Cake with Lemon–Cream Cheese Frosting

Grilled Chile-Marinated Pork Loins
with Avocado Salsa – serves 10

2 4–4½-pound pork loins

3 cups Red Chile Sauce, reserve ½ cup (see page 187 for recipe)

salt and pepper

Place the pork loins in large plastic baggie, and pour in 2½ cups Red Chile Sauce. Seal the bag, and marinate at room temperature for 1 hour or refrigerate and marinate for 4 hours. Return pork to room temperature before cooking.

Preheat grill to medium-high. Lightly brush or spray the grill rack with vegetable oil. Remove pork loins from the baggie, brushing off excess sauce. Place loins on grill, sprinkle with salt and pepper, close lid, and cook for 15 minutes. Turn the pork loins over, brush remaining ½ cup sauce on both, sprinkle with salt and pepper, close the grill lid, and continue to cook for 15 minutes or until loins are evenly browned and firm to the touch. Remove from grill, cover with foil, and let sit for 10 minutes before carving.

Avocado Salsa – serves 10

5 ripe avocados

½ fresh pineapple, cut into small pieces

3 jalapeños, seeded, deveined, and finely diced

1 bunch fresh cilantro, coarsely chopped

½ red onion, diced

fresh juice of 1 lime

½ teaspoon rice wine vinegar

salt and freshly ground pepper

Peel, pit, and coarsely chop avocados into small, bite-size pieces. Place in medium-size bowl. Add pineapple, jalapeños, cilantro, onion, lime juice, and rice wine vinegar. Blend ingredients together, being careful not to mash the avocados. Add salt and pepper to taste and serve immediately.

Oven-Roasted Sweet Potatoes – serves 10

5 large sweet potatoes

5 tablespoons butter, melted

5 tablespoons extra-virgin olive oil

2 tablespoons chile flakes

salt and pepper

Preheat oven to 350°F. Peel sweet potatoes, slice in half, then cut into 1-inch slices. Place in bowl of cool water until ready to bake. Drain potatoes and layer in a 13 x 9" baking dish. Melt butter in small sauce pan, remove from heat. Add olive oil, chile flakes, salt, and pepper. Gently whisk to blend. Pour liquid mixture over potatoes. Tightly cover baking dish with foil and bake in oven for 15 minutes. Remove foil and continue cooking for additional 10 minutes. Serve immediately.

Asparagus with Lemon and Garlic – serves 10

4 bunches fresh asparagus, trimmed

juice and zest of 4 lemons, divided into four portions

8 garlic cloves, peeled

8 tablespoons extra-virgin olive oil

Preheat oven to 325°F. Tear out 4 sheets of aluminum foil approximately 18 inches long. Place one bunch of trimmed asparagus on half of each piece of foil. Pour a quarter of the lemon juice and zest over each asparagus bunch. Press 2 garlic cloves over each, using a garlic press. Drizzle each bunch with 2 tablespoons of olive oil. Fold foil over in the middle, and crimp the edges to form an air-tight packet. Place packets directly on oven racks and bake for 15 minutes. Remove from oven and carefully open packets just before serving.

Carrot Cake with Lemon–Cream Cheese Frosting – serves 12 to 24

2 cups flour

2 cups sugar

2 tablespoons baking soda

2 teaspoons cinnamon

1 cup corn oil

3 eggs, lightly beaten

2 teaspoons vanilla

⅓ cup carrots, cooked and coarsely mashed

1 cup walnuts, chopped

1 cup shredded coconut

¾ cup drained, canned crushed pineapple

powdered sugar

Preheat oven to 350°F. Grease and flour 13 x 9 x 2" baking pan. Then line bottom of pan with wax paper. Mix flour, sugar, baking soda, and cinnamon together in large bowl. Combine oil, eggs, and vanilla in small bowl and whisk until just blended. Add oil-egg mixture to dry ingredients and beat well to moisten. Fold in carrots, walnuts, coconut, and pineapple. Pour batter into pan and bake approximately 1 hour or until edges of cake begin to pull away from sides of pan and toothpick comes out clean. Cool cake in pan on cooling rack for 10 minutes, then invert over cooling rack and unmold. Remove wax paper and let cool for 1 hour.

Frost sides and top of cake and dust with powdered sugar.

Lemon–Cream Cheese Frosting

4 ounces cream cheese, room temperature

3 tablespoons unsalted butter, room temperature

1½ cups powdered sugar (may need more to thicken frosting)

½ teaspoon vanilla

½ cup fresh lemon juice

Beat cream cheese and butter together until well blended. Slowly sift in powdered sugar and beat until smooth and no lumps remain. Stir in vanilla and lemon juice. Adjust consistency by adding more powdered sugar if necessary. Cover and set aside until cake is ready to frost.

Thursday – Day Five
Breakfast

Apple Clafouti

Bacon

Fresh Berry Bowl

Apple Clafouti – makes 8 small servings

¾ cup all-purpose flour

¼ teaspoon salt

½ cup granulated sugar

½ cup milk

2 eggs

2 tablespoons butter

6 tart apples (such as Granny Smith), peeled, cored, halved, and cut into ¼-inch slices

½ cup raisins

1 teaspoon grated lemon zest

confectioners' sugar

Heat oven to 350°F. Lightly coat a 9" square baking dish with vegetable oil spray. In a small bowl, combine the flour, salt, and 1 tablespoon of granulated sugar. Whisk in milk, then the eggs, until the batter is smooth and free of lumps. In a medium skillet, melt the butter over medium heat, and cook the apple slices with the remaining granulated sugar until tender, about 10 minutes. Mix in the raisins and lemon zest and transfer to baking dish. Pour the batter over the apples and bake for 40 minutes or until puffed and golden.

Sprinkle with confectioners' sugar and serve warm. To go along with this sweet dish, offer bacon or sausage. To finish, offer small bowls of berries or melon balls.

Lunch

Corn Chipotle Soup
Pepper Jack Quesadillas with Scallions and Black Beans
Biscochitos

Corn Chipotle Soup – serves 6

1 32-ounce package frozen corn kernels

¼ cup water

1 tablespoon butter

1 small onion, coarsely chopped

1 clove garlic, chopped

2 cups chicken broth

1 tablespoon Bufalo brand chipotle sauce (or other hot sauce)

salt and pepper to taste

Thaw corn. In small batches, purée corn until smooth, adding water (sparingly) if mixture becomes too thick. Press through sieve to remove solids. Set purée aside. Melt butter in medium sauté pan over medium heat. Add onion and garlic and cook until softened. Purée onion-garlic mixture with ½ cup corn purée, until smooth. Pour purée, onion-garlic mixture, and chicken broth into stock pot. Bring to a simmer and add the hot sauce, salt, and pepper. Simmer another 5 minutes and serve.

Pepper Jack Quesadillas with Scallions and Black Beans – serves 10

8 tablespoons salted butter

2 14-ounce cans black beans, drained and rinsed several times

20 medium-size flour tortillas

8 scallions, thinly sliced

1 pound pepper jack cheese, finely grated

Melt several teaspoons of butter in a heavy-duty skillet or flat griddle. Dump the rinsed and drained beans into a shallow bowl and roughly mash them. Take 10 tortillas and spread each one with 3 tablespoons of mashed black beans. Sprinkle 2 teaspoons of scallions on top of the beans; then lightly cover the scallions with cheese. Top with a second tortilla and carefully place in skillet or griddle. Fry the quesadilla until lightly browned, about 4 minutes. Then flip over and cook again until cheese is melted and the tortilla is nicely browned on both sides. Remove and place in 200°F oven until all the quesadillas are cooked. Cut each quesadilla into quarters, and fan the 4 wedges on the side of each plate.

Biscochitos –
makes approximately 5 dozen

1 pound lard

1 cup sugar

2 eggs

⅔ cup orange juice

½ teaspoon salt

3 teaspoons baking powder

6 cups flour

3 teaspoons anise seed

1 cup sugar and ¼ cup cinnamon, mixed together

Preheat oven to 400°F. Mix first eight ingredients together with large spoon, adding the anise seed last. Chill for at least 30 minutes. Cut out cookies, using a 2" round cookie cutter; then dredge in the sugar/cinnamon mixture. Place on cookie sheet. Bake for 10 minutes or until light brown.

A sweet-tart fruit sorbet brings out the best in these traditional cookies.

Dinner

Spicy Seared Salmon with Thai Vegetables and Sweet Rice

Oranges in Lemon Juice

Chocolate Caramel Tart

Salmon Seasoning

prepare in advance

- 2 teaspoons chile powder
- 2 teaspoons pepper flakes
- 2 teaspoons curry powder
- 2 teaspoons ground coriander
- 2 teaspoons ground cumin
- 2 teaspoons dry mustard
- 2 teaspoons salt
- 2 teaspoons sugar
- 8 6–7-ounce salmon fillets with skin

Mix chile powder, pepper flakes, curry, coriander, cumin, mustard, salt, and sugar in small bowl to blend. Cover rimmed cooking sheet with foil, and place salmon fillets on it, skin side down. Sprinkle 1½ teaspoons of spice mixture over each fillet. Cover with plastic and refrigerate 3 hours or overnight.

Spicy Seared Salmon with Thai Vegetables and Sweet Rice – serves 8

The rice, vegetables, and dressing are prepared individually but simultaneously.

Sweet Rice

- 1 tablespoon butter
- 2 cups basmati rice
- 2 cups water
- ⅓ cup canned coconut milk, unsweetened

Melt butter in large saucepan over medium heat; add rice and sauté until rice is coated, about 2 minutes. Add water and coconut milk and bring to a boil. Cover and reduce heat to low, cooking until rice is cooked and liquid is absorbed, about 20–25 minutes. Let rest, covered, for 10 minutes.

Fluff gently with fork just before serving.

Thai Vegetables

- 2 tablespoons sesame oil
- 4 teaspoons fresh ginger, peeled and minced
- 2 large garlic cloves, minced
- 2 large red bell peppers, cut into lengthwise strips
- 12 ounces shiitake mushrooms, stemmed and thinly sliced
- 6 green onions, thinly sliced on the diagonal
- 6 cups thinly sliced bok choy (approximately 2 bunches, green leaf tops only)

salt and pepper

Heat sesame oil in heavy, large skillet over high heat. Add ginger and garlic, sautéing for 20 seconds. Add bell peppers and mushrooms. Sauté until peppers are tender crisp, about 3 minutes. Add green onions and bok choy and sauté 2 minutes or until just wilted. Season with salt and pepper.

Spicy Dressing

12 tablespoons rice vinegar

6 tablespoons soy sauce

4 tablespoons sesame oil

4 tablespoons chopped fresh cilantro

2 tablespoons fresh ginger, peeled and chopped

2 teaspoons sugar

Whisk all ingredients together and set aside.

Seared Salmon

salmon fillets

4 tablespoons vegetable oil

Heat vegetable oil in large skillet over medium-high until oil simmers. Add salmon fillets, in batches, flesh side down. Sear until brown and crisp, about 5 minutes. Turn over fillets, and sear skin side until salmon is just cooked through, another 3 minutes. Remove from skillet and keep warm.

Spoon rice on individual plates. Top each serving with a salmon fillet, then vegetables. Drizzle dressing over all and serve immediately, with extra dressing on the side.

Oranges in Lemon Juice –
serves 10

5 oranges, peeled, sectioned, and cut into bite-size pieces (reserve the juice)

juice of $\frac{1}{2}$ lemon

zest of $\frac{1}{2}$ lemon

$\frac{1}{2}$ teaspoon sugar

2 heads red leaf lettuce

Mix the reserved orange juice, lemon juice, lemon zest, and sugar together in a small bowl. Pour over the pieces of orange and let sit for $\frac{1}{2}$ hour. Wash and dry lettuce leaves. Distribute evenly among the 10 plates. With slotted spoon, divide the orange pieces evenly and put on top of the lettuce leaves. Pour a bit of the juice mixture over each salad and serve immediately.

Chocolate Caramel Tart – serves 10–12

This recipe has two parts, the chocolate pâté sucrée crust and the tart filling.

Chocolate Pâté Sucrée

1¼ cups all-purpose flour

2 tablespoons cocoa powder

⅓ cup sugar

½ teaspoon salt

6 tablespoons unsalted butter, chilled and cut into pieces

3 large egg yolks

½ teaspoons pure vanilla extract

1 cup pecans, chopped

Place the flour, cocoa, sugar, and salt in the bowl of a food processor and pulse several times to combine. Add the butter and pulse until the mixture resembles coarse meal, about 10 seconds. Add egg yolks and vanilla and process just until mixture begins to hold together, no more than 30 seconds. Turn dough out onto a lightly floured surface and form into a disk. Cover in plastic wrap and refrigerate for 30 minutes or until ready to use.

When ready to begin baking, preheat oven to 350°F. Roll chocolate pâté sucrée ⅛ inch thick and fit into a 9" fluted tart pan with a removable bottom. Prick bottom of tart with a fork. Refrigerate the shell for 30 minutes. Place the chopped pecans on a baking sheet and toast until slightly darkened and fragrant, about 10 minutes. Set aside. Line tart shell with parchment paper, pressing into edges, and cover with dried beans or pie weights. Place on a baking sheet and bake for 20 minutes. Remove paper and beans, and continue baking until crust is golden, about 10 minutes. Transfer to a wire rack to cool completely.

Tart Filling

1 cup sugar

¼ teaspoon salt

¼ cup water

1½ cups heavy cream

2 tablespoons unsalted butter, room temperature

1 teaspoon pure vanilla extract

6 ounces bittersweet chocolate, finely chopped

cocoa, for dusting (optional)

caramel-dipped pecans (optional)

To make caramel, place sugar, salt, and water in a small saucepan. Bring this mixture to a boil over medium-high heat. When it reaches a boil, wash down the sides of the pan with a pastry brush dipped in water (to prevent crystals from forming). Cook gently, swirling pan (do not stir), until the caramel is a rich amber color. Remove from heat and add ½ cup cream, butter, and vanilla. Stir until smooth. Pour mixture into chocolate tart shell. Sprinkle the roasted pecans over the top and place in the refrigerator while melting the chocolate.

Place chocolate in a medium heat-proof bowl. Bring remaining cup of cream to a boil in a small saucepan and pour over the chocolate. Let sit for 5 minutes, then stir until completely smooth. Pour over caramel and nuts and return tart to refrigerator to chill for at least 1 hour. Dust top of the tart with cocoa powder and caramel-dipped pecans before serving.

Friday – Day Six
(Farewell)
Continental Breakfast

English Muffins, Bagels, Cream Cheese,
Fruit Jam, Orange Juice,
Fresh Melon Slices,
Yogurt, Granola, and Coffee and Tea

Now every field is clothed with grass,
and every tree with leaves;
now the woods put forth their blossoms,
and the year assumes its gay attire.

— Virgil

Summer

In summer, the song sings itself.

— *William Carlos Williams*

Summer in Santa Fe brings dry, beautiful days in the eighties and cool evenings in the fifties—and a bounty of activities to enjoy under a majestic azure sky. Nestled in the foothills of the Rocky Mountains, rimmed by the spectacular Sangre de Cristo Mountains, Santa Fe is a culturally rich city offering world-class visual and performing arts alongside a wide range of walks and hikes boasting both spectacular views and fragments of the deep past of today's Pueblo peoples. June, July, and August bring the annual Santa Fe Plaza Arts and Crafts Festival, the Eight Northern Indian Pueblos Artist and Craftsman Show, Spanish Market, and the renowned Santa Fe Indian Market, to name only a few. The Santa Fe Opera is in full swing in its soaring mountain-top concert hall, and Maria Benitez and other groups thrill the city with inspiring musical performances. Conversations fill the air with an exotic mix of English, Navajo, Keres, Spanish, and Zuni—not to mention German, French, and Japanese.

In early June, mountain meadows may be blanketed with tiny wild irises. As summer unfolds, hollyhocks, wild asters, sunflowers, and an occasional spiky buffalo gourd, among many others, bloom along roadsides and in mountain dells. It's a bird-watcher's paradise: broadtail and rufous hummingbirds, tree swallows, mountain bluebirds, robins, juncos, Stellar's bluejays, woodpeckers, and even the occasional dove owl roost and fly in the trees that line the city's waterways. Thunderstorms, common in summer, stage their dramatic interplay of thunder and

lightning against billowing gray and lavender clouds, frequently followed by shimmering rainbows and watercolor sunsets.

A Santa Fe summer is as sweet as the juice of the season's first strawberry, as cooling as a plaza stroll while licking a double-dip, chocolate ice cream cone, and as salty and delectable as roasted corn on the cob fresh off the grill. The enveloping atmosphere of this unique environment is stimulating and supportive for scholar and artist alike. Creativity is on the wind, and the School for Advanced Research plays midwife to a host of deeply considered ideas and a truly interactive, innovative community.

WELCOME DINNER
Saturday

Oven-Fried Chicken

Potato Salad

Green Beans with Lemon-Butter Sauce

Vanilla Ice Cream with Gana's Hot Fudge Sauce

Oven-Fried Chicken – serves 12

3 boxes plain Melba toast

6 large eggs

3 tablespoons Dijon mustard

3 teaspoons dried thyme

2¼ teaspoons salt

1½ teaspoons coarsely ground pepper

1½ teaspoons dried oregano

¾ teaspoon garlic powder

¾ teaspoon cayenne or chipotle powder

¾ cup vegetable oil

4 chicken breasts, split, skinned, and patted dry

8 whole chicken leg quarters, separated into drumsticks and thighs, skinned, and patted dry

Preheat oven to 400°F and set racks to middle positions, leaving room between racks for heat to circulate. Place Melba toasts in a large baggie and pound with meat pounder until they resemble coarse sand with some small pebble-size pieces. Do NOT pulverize. Pour crumbs in shallow pie tin. Line rimmed baking sheet with foil, and set large wire cooling rack over baking sheet. Mix eggs, mustard, thyme, salt, pepper, oregano, garlic powder, and cayenne powder in shallow dish. Stir with a small whisk or fork to blend. Drizzle oil over Melba toast crumbs and toss well to coat. Working with one piece of chicken at a time, dip the chicken on both sides into the egg mixture. Roll in the crumbs and press to coat, making sure that the piece is well coated. Gently shake off excess crumbs, and place pieces (what would normally be the skin side up) on wire rack. Do not crowd the chicken! Bake for 40 minutes or until chicken is deep nutty brown and juices run clear.

Potato Salad – serves 10

2 pounds Yukon Gold potatoes

¼ cup white wine vinegar

¼ cup extra-virgin olive oil

½ teaspoon salt

½ teaspoon freshly ground pepper

½ cup red onion, thinly sliced

½ cup celery, thinly sliced

1½ cucumbers, peeled, seeded, cut into quarters, and sliced

1 tablespoon fresh lemon juice

1 cup mayonnaise

½ cup sour cream

2½ cups Dijon mustard

10 hardboiled eggs (optional)

1 cup fresh Italian parsley, chopped

Place potatoes in large pot of salted water and bring to boil. Cook until tender but still firm. Drain and rinse in cold water. Peel as soon as potatoes are cool enough to handle, and roughly slice into bite-size pieces. Sprinkle warm potatoes with vinegar, olive oil, salt, and pepper. Add red onion, celery, and cucumbers. In separate bowl, combine lemon juice, mayonnaise, sour cream, and mustard. Whisk to mix well. Pour over vegetable mixture and gently toss to coat thoroughly. Cool to room temperature, cover tightly, and refrigerate overnight. Before serving, add eggs and parsley, tossing gently to combine. Add more mayonnaise if potatoes are dry.

Serve with garnish of parsley sprigs.

Green Beans with Lemon-Butter Sauce – serves 10

1½ pounds green beans, trimmed

1 lemon

3 tablespoons butter

salt and pepper to taste

Cook beans in large pot of salted, boiling water until crisp tender and vibrant green, about 5 minutes. Drain and run under cold water. Using vegetable peeler, cut off lemon peel in strips. Slice strips very thinly. Melt butter in large skillet over medium-high heat. Add 1½ teaspoons lemon peel and sauté until fragrant. Add beans and toss with lemon-butter mixture until heated through. Season with salt and pepper and serve immediately.

Gana's Hot Fudge Sauce – makes 2–2½ cups

1⅓ cups sweet condensed milk

2 ounces unsweetened chocolate

½ teaspoon salt

¾ cup water

¾ teaspoon vanilla

Fill one third of the bottom of a double boiler with water. Bring to a boil. Combine milk, chocolate, and salt in top of double boiler and cook until very thick, stirring constantly. Remove from heat and gradually add the water. Stir to mix well. Let mixture cool slightly, and add vanilla. Bring mixture to room temperature, then refrigerate in air-tight container until ready to use. May be reheated before use.

Serve over a fine French vanilla ice cream.

Sunday – Day One
Breakfast

Blueberry-Stuffed French Toast

Sausage

Watermelon Wedges

Blueberry-Stuffed French Toast – serves 9

1 14-ounce loaf challah (egg) bread

4 ounces cream cheese

3 cups blueberries, divided in two

8 eggs, beaten

1½ cups milk

¼ cup maple syrup

¼ cup butter, melted

½ teaspoon vanilla

Preheat oven to 350°F. Grease 9 x 9 x 2" baking dish. Remove crust from bread and cut into 1-inch cubes (should make 10 cups). Cut cream cheese into small cubes, about 1 cup. Place half the bread cubes in baking dish and sprinkle with cream cheese and 1½ cups blueberries. Repeat for second layer. Combine eggs, milk, syrup, melted butter, and vanilla in separate bowl and carefully pour over bread-cream cheese mixture. Bake 1 hour or until knife inserted in middle comes out clean.

Cut into squares and serve with additional syrup. This dish is delicious when served with spicy sausage and wedges of juicy watermelon on the side.

Lunch

Tuna Salad on Butter Lettuce

Cheese Cornbread with Pepitas

Pecan-Chocolate Squares

Cheese Cornbread with Pepitas –
serves 10

1 cup cornmeal

1 cup creamed corn

¾ cup buttermilk

⅓ cup vegetable oil

2 eggs, slightly beaten

½ teaspoon baking soda

1 teaspoon salt

1½ cups grated cheddar cheese

1 cup toasted pepitas (shelled pumpkin seeds)

Preheat oven to 350°F. Butter 8 x 8" square baking dish, or use a 9" round skillet at least 2" deep. Mix cornmeal, corn, buttermilk, oil, eggs, baking soda, and salt together. Fold in cheese and pepitas. Bake for 40 minutes.

Tuna Salad on Butter Lettuce – serves 8

12 ounces canned Spanish tuna in water (or Albacore)

1 cup red bell pepper, chopped

1½ cups fresh pineapple, coarsely chopped

3 cloves garlic, finely chopped

1 cup red onion, finely diced

⅓ cup fresh Italian parsley, coarsely chopped

¼ cup fresh basil, finely chopped

6 tablespoons fresh lemon juice

2 cups mayonnaise

2 tablespoons fresh oregano, chopped

salt and freshly ground pepper to taste

2 heads each butter and red leaf lettuce

almonds, toasted and slivered, to taste

Drain tuna and rinse well with water. Combine with red pepper, pineapple, garlic, onion, parsley, and basil. Add lemon juice. Toss gently to combine. In separate bowl, whisk mayonnaise with oregano, salt, and pepper until well blended. Pour over tuna mixture and toss to mix well. Cover and refrigerate.

Serve on bed of butter and red lettuce and sprinkle with toasted almond slivers.

Pecan-Chocolate Squares –
makes sixteen 2½-inch squares*

Cookie Base

¾ cup cold unsalted butter, cut into ½-inch cubes

2 cups flour

½ cup light brown sugar, packed

2 teaspoons cinnamon

½ teaspoon salt

¾ cup finely grated bittersweet chocolate

Heat oven to 350°F, and place rack in middle position. Prepare base first. Put the butter, flour, light brown sugar, cinnamon, and salt in food processor. Pulse 20 times or until mixture is well combined. Scatter the dough into a 9 x 12" baking pan and press evenly over the bottom. Bake until firm and lightly browned, about 25 minutes. When cookie base comes out of the oven, quickly sprinkle the grated chocolate evenly over the top. Set the pan aside.

Pecan Topping

3 cups toasted pecans

½ cup unsalted butter

1 cup dark brown sugar, packed

⅓ cup honey

2 tablespoons heavy cream

½ teaspoon salt

As the cookie base bakes, pulse the pecans in the processor until coarsely chopped. Melt butter in medium-size heavy sauce pan. Stir in dark brown sugar, honey, cream, and salt. Simmer for 1 minute. Add pecans. Pour the pecan mixture over the base, spreading evenly. Bake until much of the filling is bubbling (not just the sides), about 16–18 minutes. Let cool completely in pan.

*Tightly covered, these bars will keep for 5 days.

Dinner

Spinach Lasagne

Green Salad with Balsamic Vinaigrette

Apricot-Ginger Cobbler

Spinach Lasagne – serves 10

3 tablespoons canola oil

1 cup onion, finely chopped

4 garlic cloves, minced

1 2-pound package of fresh baby spinach

½ teaspoon salt

¼ teaspoon freshly ground pepper

1½ teaspoons dried mustard

2½ cups cottage cheese, drained

2 teaspoons nutmeg

2 cups prepared marinara sauce

1 pound no-cook lasagna noodles

6 cups mozzarella cheese, grated and divided into fourths

1½ cups shredded parmesan cheese

Preheat oven to 375°F. Heat canola oil in large sauté pan. Add the onion and garlic, cooking over medium heat until golden brown. Stir in the spinach, salt, pepper, and mustard, mixing well. Cover, reduce heat to low, and cook until spinach is just limp. Remove from heat. Mix drained cottage cheese with nutmeg in a separate bowl. Spread ½ cup marinara sauce in deep 9 x 13" baking dish. Top with layer of lasagna noodles, ¾ cup of the cottage cheese mixture, 1½ cups mozzarella cheese, ½ cup parmesan cheese, and a third of the spinach mixture. Repeat two more times and top with remaining marinara sauce. Cover tightly with foil and bake for 30 minutes. Top with remaining 1½ cups mozzarella and bake an additional 5 minutes or until hot and bubbly. Let sit for 20 minutes before cutting into squares.

Balsamic Vinaigrette –
(see page 9)

Serve over fresh greens.

Apricot-Ginger Cobbler – serves 12

5 pounds apricots, pitted and cut into quarters

3 teaspoons ginger, pressed in garlic press

2¼ cups sugar, divided into ¾-cup and 1½-cup portions

1½ cups plus 2 tablespoons flour

2¼ teaspoons baking powder

½ teaspoon salt

¼ teaspoon baking soda

4 large eggs

¼ cup whole milk

3 tablespoons triple sec (or orange juice concentrate)

1¼ teaspoons vanilla extract

¾ teaspoon almond extract

6 tablespoons unsalted butter, melted

whipping cream or French vanilla ice cream

Preheat oven to 325°F. Mix apricots and ginger with ¾ cup sugar. Toss with 2 tablespoons flour to coat well. Transfer mixture to 13 x 9 x 2" glass baking dish. Bake until bubbling, about 15 minutes. Whisk remaining 1½ cups sugar and 1½ cups flour, baking powder, salt, and baking soda in large bowl. Whisk eggs with milk, triple sec, and vanilla and almond extracts in medium bowl. Add to dry ingredients and whisk until smooth. Fold in melted butter. Pour batter over hot apricot mixture. Continue baking until topping is brown and tester comes out clean, about 45 minutes.

Cool slightly and serve with dollop of slightly sweetened whipped cream or French vanilla ice cream.

Monday – Day Two
Continental Breakfast

English Muffins, Bagels,
Cream Cheese, Fruit Jam,
Orange Juice, Fresh Melon Slices,
Yogurt, Granola, and Coffee and Tea

Lunch

Couscous with Currants, Fresh Green Beans,
Red Onion, and Feta Cheese
Watermelon Slices with Cookies

Couscous with Currants, Fresh Green Beans, Red Onion, and Feta Cheese – serves 10

3 boxes plain couscous

¾ cup dried Zante currants

1 pound fresh green beans, washed and cut into quarters

½ pound cherry tomatoes, cut in half

½ large red onion, diced

1 cup extra-virgin olive oil

¼ cup crumbled feta cheese

Cook couscous according to package directions, adding the currants at the same time you add the couscous to the boiling water. Cook, then let cool for 30 minutes. Bring a medium pot of water to boil. Add the green beans and cook for only 3 minutes. Drain the beans in a colander and rinse several times with cold water to stop the cooking process. Gently fluff the couscous-currant mixture with a large fork, and add the cooled green beans, tomatoes, and onion. Pour the olive oil over this mix and gently stir with fork until well mixed. Refrigerate, covered, until ready to serve.

Sprinkle feta cheese over the salad at the time of serving.

Serve this salad with flat or pita bread rounds. For dessert, offer your favorite cookies with slices of watermelon.

Dinner

Roasted Leg of Lamb with Salsa Verde

Oven-Roasted Baby Potatoes with Capers and Rosemary

Baby Spinach Salad with Mango

Cheesecake

Roast Leg of Lamb with Salsa Verde – serves 6–8

Salsa Verde

1 cup extra-virgin olive oil

½ cup Italian parsley, chopped

⅓ cup green onions, finely chopped

¼ cup fresh mint

¼ cup capers, drained and chopped

1 teaspoon grated lemon peel

1 teaspoon salt

½ teaspoon pepper flakes

¾ teaspoon coarsely ground black pepper

2 tablespoons minced garlic

Stir all ingredients into large bowl. Set aside.

Lamb

1 5–6-pound leg of spring lamb, trimmed and butterflied

Place lamb on clean work surface, smooth side down, and sprinkle with salt and pepper. Rub ¼ cup of the Salsa Verde into the lamb. Roll the lamb and, using kitchen string, tie the roll together every 2 inches. Place on rimmed baking sheet and chill for 24 hours.

Remove lamb from refrigerator and let sit for 2 hours. Preheat oven to 450°F. Place lamb on rack in roasting pan and cook for 1 hour and 20 minutes for medium-rare (meat thermometer should register 125°F when inserted into thickest part of roll). Let meat rest for 15 minutes before carving. Cut crosswise into thin slices, and spoon salsa over each slice. Remaining salsa should be put on the table.

Oven-Roasted Baby Potatoes with Capers and Rosemary – serves 8

4 pounds assorted baby potatoes

¼ cup extra-virgin olive oil

7 sprigs fresh rosemary

4 large garlic cloves, halved

1½ teaspoons sea salt

3 tablespoons capers (rinsed if in brine)

Preheat oven to 400°F. Wash and dry potatoes. Cut in half and arrange in single layer on large rimmed baking sheet. Drizzle with oil. Break 3 of the rosemary sprigs into 4 pieces each and sprinkle over potatoes, along with garlic and salt. Gently toss to coat. Stirring every 15 minutes, roast until potatoes just begin to turn tender, about 40 minutes. Mix in capers and roast for another 5 minutes. Transfer to plates and garnish with remaining 4 rosemary sprigs.

Cheesecake – serves 10

48 ounces cream cheese (4 blocks), room temperature

4 eggs, room temperature

1¼ cups sugar

1 tablespoon fresh lemon juice

1 tablespoon lemon zest

2 teaspoons vanilla

Preheat oven to 350°F. Place rack in middle position. Blend all ingredients together with electric blender until very smooth. Pour into buttered springform pan. Bake 60–70 minutes or until top is light brown and cake has pulled away from sides of pan. Remove from oven and let stand 15 minutes.

Pour topping (see sidebar) over warm cake. Return to oven and continue baking for 10 minutes. Remove and cool completely before covering tightly and refrigerating for 24 hours.

Baby Spinach Salad with Mango –
serves 10

1 14-ounce package baby spinach

5 ripe mangoes, peeled and cut into bite-size pieces

Divide the cleaned and stemmed baby spinach among 10 plates. Spoon the mango pieces over the spinach, and drizzle the remaining mango juice over the salads. Serve immediately.

Cheesecake Topping

While cake is baking, mix until smooth:

2 cups sour cream

¼ cup sugar

1 teaspoon vanilla

Tuesday – Day Three
Breakfast

Spanish Torta with Red Chile Sauce

Bacon

Fresh Berry Bowl

Spanish Torta with Red Chile Sauce – serves 8

Red Chile Sauce
(see page 187)

Spanish Torta

4 tablespoons olive oil

2 onions, peeled, halved, and each half thinly sliced crosswise

4 pounds thin-skinned potatoes, peeled and sliced into ⅛-inch-thick rounds

1½ teaspoons salt

1 teaspoon pepper

⅔ cup water

10 large eggs

Heat olive oil in two ovenproof 10–12" skillets over medium-high heat; when hot, add one half of onion to each, cooking and stirring often until limp, about 5 minutes. Add potatoes, ½ teaspoon salt, and ¼ teaspoon pepper to each pan and mix to coat. Add ⅓ cup water to each pan and bring to a boil. Reduce heat to medium, cover, and cook until potatoes are tender when pierced, about 10 minutes. If any liquid remains in pan, boil uncovered until evaporated, 1–2 minutes. Meanwhile, in a large bowl, beat eggs with ½ teaspoon salt and ½ teaspoon pepper to blend. Add potato mixture and mix gently. Place unwashed frying pans over medium heat; when hot, pour in egg-potato mixture. Reduce heat to medium-low and cook until eggs begin to set and bottom is lightly browned, about 5–8 minutes. Transfer pans to oven, and broil tortas about 6 inches from heat until top is set, 3–5 minutes. Run spatula between torta and pan to loosen; invert tortas onto a plate.

Cut into 8–10 wedges and serve warm or at room temperature, with salsa on the side.

Bacon and fresh berries are the perfect companions for this torta.

Lunch

Chicken Noodle Soup with Rosemary and Spinach

Carla's Tres Leches Cake

Chicken Noodle Soup with Rosemary and Spinach – serves 10

4 cups cooked wide egg noodles

1 tablespoon olive oil

2½ teaspoons salt

8 cups water

4 cups chicken broth

2 cups chopped onion

1 cup chopped celery

2 tablespoons dried rosemary

1½ pounds boneless and skinless chicken breasts

1½ pounds boneless and skinless chicken thighs

1½ cups coarsely grated carrots

1 cup sliced mushrooms

⅓ cup fresh parsley, finely chopped

2 cups baby spinach leaves

½ cup fresh lemon juice

½ tablespoon freshly ground pepper

Cook noodles according to directions (do not overcook!). Rinse and set aside. Combine cooked noodles, oil, and ½ teaspoon salt. Toss to coat well and set aside. Combine water, chicken broth, onion, celery, rosemary, 1 teaspoon salt, and chicken in large stock pot. Bring to a boil. Cover, reduce heat to simmer, and cook 30 minutes. Remove chicken and set aside until it is cool enough to shred. Then add shredded chicken, carrots, mushrooms, parsley, spinach, and 1 teaspoon salt to pot and bring back to a boil. Cover, and turn off heat. Stir in noodle mixture, lemon juice, and pepper. Simmer for 1 minute and serve immediately.

Slices of warm bread with butter go well with this hearty soup.

Carla's Tres Leches Cake – serves 10–12

1 package white cake mix

1 12-ounce can evaporated milk

1 14-ounce can condensed milk

1 7.6-ounce can Nestlé brand media crema

$\frac{1}{4}$ cup brandy or 1$\frac{1}{2}$ teaspoons almond extract

1$\frac{1}{2}$ teaspoons vanilla extract

$\frac{1}{2}$ cup coconut (optional), packed

Prepare cake batter and bake in 13 x 9 x 2" baking dish as directed on package. Cool cake in pan for 10 minutes. Pierce cake with large fork at $\frac{1}{2}$-inch intervals. With an electric blender, mix the three kinds of milk, almond extract (or brandy), vanilla extract, and coconut (if desired). Blend until smooth. Carefully pour over cake, piercing cake as needed until milk mixture is absorbed. Frost top of cake with whipped cream.

Dinner

On Tuesdays, the custom is for the president of the School
to take the seminar participants out to dinner
at one of Santa Fe's many fine restaurants.
This time of year, they may dine outside in the patio,
enjoying the fresh, cool evenings of the high desert in summer.

Wednesday – Day Four
Continental Breakfast

English Muffins, Bagels, Cream Cheese,
Fruit Jam, Orange Juice, Fresh Melon Slices,
Yogurt, Granola, and Coffee and Tea

Lunch

Pasta Salad with Artichokes and Sun-Dried Tomatoes

Coconut Macaroon Bars

Pasta Salad with Artichokes and Sun-Dried Tomatoes* – serves 6–8

1 20-ounce package fresh three-cheese tortellini

½ cup mayonnaise

½ cup olive oil

¼ cup red wine vinegar

1½ teaspoons Dijon mustard

1 teaspoon sugar

1 tablespoon salt

½ teaspoon ground black pepper

¼ teaspoon dried oregano

¼ teaspoon dried thyme

¼ teaspoon dried basil

1 garlic clove, pressed

2 cups chopped celery

1 13-ounce can artichokes in water, chopped

¾ cup chopped green onions

½ cup drained, oil-packed, sun-dried tomatoes, coarsely chopped

½ cup Kalamata olives, pitted, coarsely chopped

½ cup freshly grated parmesan cheese

Cook pasta in large pot of boiling, salted water until just tender but still firm. Drain and then rinse with cold water to cool quickly. Drain again. Whisk mayonnaise and next ten ingredients in small bowl until well blended. Transfer about ¾ cup to large bowl and mix in celery, artichokes, green onions, tomatoes, and olives. Add pasta to veggies; then add parmesan cheese. Gently toss to blend. Mix in more dressing by quarter cupfuls, if desired.

*Best if made the night before. Serve chilled or at room temperature.

Coconut Macaroon Bars – makes 24

Crust

1¼ cups flour

⅓ cup sugar

½ teaspoon salt

10 tablespoons unsalted butter, chilled and diced

1 large egg yolk

1 tablespoon whipping cream

Preheat oven to 350°F. Spray 13 x 9 x 2" metal baking pan with nonstick spray. Blend flour, cup sugar, and salt in food processor. Add diced butter and process, using on/off turns until mixture resembles coarse meal. Add egg yolk and cream, blending until dough comes together in clumps. Press dough evenly over bottom of prepared pan. Bake crust 15 minutes or until golden brown.

Filling

2 tablespoons flour

1 cup sugar

¼ teaspoon salt

3 large eggs

¼ cup unsalted butter, melted and cooled

2 teaspoons vanilla

1 7-ounce package flaked coconut

Beat flour, sugar, salt, eggs, butter, and vanilla in bowl until just blended. Add coconut and blend well. Pour filling over crust. Bake 25 minutes or until golden brown on top and set in center. Cool in pan and cut into 24 bars.

Dinner

Chiles Rellenos Casserole

Warm Flour Tortillas

Tossed Green Salad

Margarita Pie

Chiles Rellenos Casserole – serves 8

16 poblano chiles

2 cups Monterey jack cheese, grated

2 cups cheddar cheese, grated

4 teaspoons canned chipotle chiles in adobo sauce, chopped

½ cup flour

8 large eggs, separated

2 teaspoons hot sauce

½ cup canola oil

2 large eggs, lightly beaten

1 cup yellow cornmeal

2 cups sour cream

2 cups frozen creamed corn, defrosted

Preheat oven to 450°F. Place poblano chiles on a baking sheet and roast until blackened on all sides, about 20 minutes. Remove from baking sheet and place in paper bag for 20 minutes. Reduce oven temperature to 350°F. Remove the chiles from the bag, and carefully rub off the charred skin. With a sharp knife, make a slit in one side of each chile from ½ inch below the base of the stem to ½ inch from the bottom of the chile. This makes stuffing the chiles easier. Combine the cheeses and the chipotle chiles in a medium bowl. Fill the poblano chiles with the cheese mixture, and press the slit closed. Roll the chiles in flour, covering the entire chile pod.

Beat 8 egg yolks with the hot sauce in a medium-size bowl, and stir in the remaining flour. In a separate bowl, beat 8 egg whites with mixer until stiff; then gently fold the egg whites into the egg yolk mixture. Heat the canola oil in a large sauté pan. Dip the chiles into the egg mixture and sauté until golden brown on all sides, about 5 minutes. Remove from oil and place on absorbent paper towel. Continue sautéing until all chiles are done. Place all chiles side by side in two 8 x 10" baking dishes, leaving space around each chile. In a small bowl, mix the remaining 2 eggs with the cornmeal, sour cream, and creamed corn. Pour this over the chiles. Bake for 25–30 minutes or until the cornmeal mixture is set and a light golden brown.

Serve immediately with warm flour tortillas on the side. A tossed green salad with Champagne dressing (see page 189) complements this entree nicely.

Margarita Pie – serves 8

1½ cups (3.5 ounces) lightly packed marshmallows

⅔ cup half and half

1 teaspoon grated lime peel

¼ cup fresh lime juice

¼ cup tequila (silver)

20 thin chocolate wafer cookies

2 tablespoons butter, melted

1 cup whipping cream

1½ tablespoons sugar

In a 3–4-quart pan over medium heat, stir marshmallows with half and half until melted, about 5 minutes. Nest pan in ice water and stir often until cool, about 3 minutes. Add lime peel, lime juice, and tequila. Stir occasionally until cold, 8–10 minutes. In a food processor, whirl cookies until finely ground. Add butter and whirl until mixed. Press cookie mixture evenly over bottom and halfway up sides of 9-inch cake pan with removable rim. In bowl, with mixer on high speed, whip cream with sugar until it holds soft peaks. Fold in marshmallow mixture, blending well. Pour filling into crust and spread to level. Freeze until firm to touch in the center, about 1 hour. Wrap tightly and freeze, until solid, at least 2 hours or up to two weeks. Unwrap pie, run a thin knife between crust and pan rim, and remove rim. Set dessert on flat surface. Let stand at room temperature about 10 minutes to soften slightly, then cut into wedges.

Thursday—Day Five
Breakfast

Oven Pancakes with Apples

Sausage

Fresh Fruit Bowl

Oven Pancakes with Apples – serves 4–5

1 cup milk

3 large eggs, room temperature

¾ cup flour

3 tablespoons sugar

2 tablespoons butter

2 cups Granny Smith apples, peeled and cut into ¼-inch slices

2 teaspoons cinnamon

powdered sugar

lemon wedges

Preheat oven to 375°F. Whisk milk, eggs, flour, and 2 tablespoons sugar together in bowl. Set aside. Melt butter in large, oven-proof skillet. Add apples, cinnamon, and remaining 1 tablespoon sugar. Cook over medium-high heat until apples are tender. Remove from heat. Pour batter over apple mixture and place in oven. Bake 30–35 minutes.

Cut into wedges, dust with powdered sugar, and serve with lemon wedges on the side.

To accompany the pancakes, consider sausage rounds and bowls of fresh fruit or berries.

Lunch

Edamame and Black Beans with Quinoa Salad in Basil-Lime Dressing

Caramel-Nut Brownies

Edamame and Black Beans with Quinoa Salad in Basil-Lime Dressing – serves 10

Salad

1½ cups uncooked quinoa

3 cups vegetable broth

1 10-ounce package edamame beans

½ cup scallions, sliced

4 cups tomatoes, seeded and chopped

½ cup carrot, finely chopped

1 15-ounce can black beans, rinsed and drained

Combine quinoa with vegetable broth in saucepan and bring to a boil. Cover and simmer until broth is absorbed, about 15 minutes. Remove from heat. When cool, add to dressing (see below) and toss.

Cook edamame beans according to package directions. Let cool, and remove beans from pods. Discard pods. Add edamame beans, scallions, tomatoes, carrot, and black beans to quinoa mixture. Stir gently to combine. Cover and refrigerate until ready to serve.

Basil-Lime Dressing

2 tablespoons extra-virgin olive oil

1 teaspoon salt

1 cup fresh basil, chopped

3 tablespoons fresh lime juice

2 tablespoons Dijon mustard

1 teaspoon sugar

2 teaspoons grated lime zest

½ teaspoon freshly ground black pepper

4 garlic cloves, minced

Mix all dressing ingredients together in large bowl. Whisk well to blend.

Caramel-Nut Brownies – makes 12–24

1 14-ounce package caramels (about 50)
$\frac{2}{3}$ cup evaporated milk
1 German chocolate cake mix
$\frac{3}{4}$ cup unsalted butter, melted
1 cup chocolate chips
1 cup chopped pecans

Preheat oven to 350°F. Grease and flour 13 x 9 x 2" baking dish. Melt caramels with $\frac{1}{3}$ cup evaporated milk in double boiler. Keep water simmering to melt the caramels slowly. Combine cake mix with butter and $\frac{1}{3}$ cup evaporated milk and stir to mix well. Batter will be very thick. Pour half of batter into prepared dish and bake for 10 minutes. Remove from oven and sprinkle with chocolate chips and nuts. Drizzle with melted caramel mixture. Cover with remaining cake batter. Return to oven and bake additional 15 minutes or until brownies are firm to the touch.

Cool completely before cutting.

Dinner

Grilled Chicken, Red Onion, and Mint Kebabs

Greek Salad

Lemon Sabayon and Grilled Peaches

Grilled Chicken, Red Onion, and Mint Kebabs – serves 8

3 pounds skinless, boneless chicken breast halves,
   cut into 1-inch cubes

8 tablespoons extra-virgin olive oil

8 garlic cloves, crushed

2 teaspoons dried mint

2 teaspoons dried oregano

2 teaspoons salt

2 teaspoons freshly ground black pepper

4 tablespoons fresh lemon juice

2 red onions, cut into 1-inch pieces

2 bunches fresh mint

salt and pepper to taste

16 12-inch skewers (if using wood, soak beforehand
   to eliminate burning)

Mix chicken, 4 tablespoons oil, garlic, mint, oregano, salt, and pepper in medium bowl. Marinate 30 minutes. Whisk remaining 4 tablespoons oil with lemon juice in small bowl to blend. Set barbeque to medium-high heat. Alternate chicken, onion, and mint leaves on skewers. Sprinkle with salt and pepper. Grill until chicken is just cooked through, turning and basting occasionally with oil-lemon mixture, about 9 minutes.

Greek Salad – serves 10*

1½ pounds tomatoes, seeded, diced (about 4 cups)

4 cups cucumber (2 large), diced, seeded, and peeled

3 cups diced red bell pepper (2 large)

½ cup pitted Kalamata olives or other brine-cured black olives, halved

½ cup diced red onion

6 tablespoons chopped fresh Italian parsley

3 tablespoons red wine vinegar

1 teaspoon dried oregano

½ cup crumbled feta cheese (about 8 ounces)

salt and pepper to taste

Toss everything but the feta cheese in a medium bowl to blend. Gently mix in cheese. Season with salt and pepper. Let stand at room temperature before serving

*Can be made 2 hours ahead.

Lemon Sabayon – serves 8

10 large egg yolks

⅔ cup plus 2 tablespoons sugar

⅔ cup champagne or sparkling wine

4 tablespoons fresh lemon juice

1½ cups heavy cream, chilled

1 teaspoon grated lemon zest

Prepare an ice bath and set aside. Combine yolks, sugar, champagne, and lemon juice in a large metal bowl. Set over a large pan of simmering water. Whisk until mixture is very thick and has expanded in volume. Place bowl in ice bath and let cool completely. Place cream in large bowl and beat until stiff peaks form. Fold whipped cream into egg yolk mixture. Gently fold in lemon zest. Cover with plastic wrap and place in refrigerator for at least 20 minutes.

Divide Sabayon among 8 dishes, and top each with a peach half.

Grilled Peaches

4 peaches, halved and pitted

4 tablespoons unsalted butter, melted

4 tablespoons light brown sugar

Line grill or pan with heavy-duty foil. Brush peaches with melted butter and sprinkle with brown sugar. Grill cut side down, until peaches are tender and sugar is caramelized, about 6–7 minutes.

Friday – Day Six
Farewell
Continental Breakfast

English Muffins, Bagels, Cream Cheese,
Fruit Jam, Orange Juice, Fresh Melon Slices,
Yogurt, Granola, and Coffee and Tea

Summer afternoon—summer afternoon;
to me those have always been the two most
beautiful words in the English language.

— Henry James

Salsas, Sauces, Dressings, and Desserts

This section became necessary after I looked through the recipes included in the main text and noticed that in designing menus, I had had to leave out many of the seminarians' favorites. Working toward providing the absolute best of everything here at SAR, I decided that the following recipes were just too good not to be included. *Enjoy!*

Salsas

Black Bean, Corn, and Tomato Salsa – makes approximately 2 cups

$\frac{2}{3}$ cup red onion, finely chopped

$\frac{1}{2}$ teaspoon garlic, minced

2 tablespoons extra-virgin olive oil

4 tablespoons coarsely chopped cilantro (may substitute Italian flat-leaf parsley)

$\frac{1}{4}$ teaspoon cumin seed, toasted and ground with a mortar and pestle

1 jalapeño, deveined and seeded, coarsely minced

2 tablespoons cider or rice vinegar

2 teaspoons red chile powder

2 tablespoons honey

1 cup cooked black beans (canned beans work just fine—just drain and rinse well)

2 fresh ears white or yellow corn, kernels removed

4 large Roma or heirloom tomatoes, coarsely chopped

Saute the onion and garlic in the olive oil, over medium heat, until the mixture is soft and slightly golden. Place the cilantro, cumin, jalapeño, vinegar, chile powder, and honey in a medium-size bowl and combine well. (Heat the honey in a microwave for 15 seconds beforehand, as heating will make it easier to blend.) Add the cooked onion, garlic, black beans, corn, and tomatoes. Toss together to coat the vegetables evenly. Set aside, covered, for 30 minutes at room temperature before serving. May be covered and refrigerated for 2 hours.

Bring back to room temperature before serving.

Roasted Tomatillo-Mango Salsa – makes approximately 2½ cups

1½ pounds fresh tomatillos

1 jalapeño

1 onion, peeled and quartered

4 garlic cloves, unpeeled

½ cup cilantro leaves, coarsely chopped

1 tablespoon fresh lime juice

1 teaspoon salt

3 cups fresh mango, diced

Clean the tomatillos, discarding husks and stems. Remove stem from jalapeño. Place tomatillos, jalapeño, onion, and garlic on rimmed cooking sheet lightly coated with olive oil. Broil 8 minutes or until the tomatillos and onions are slightly charred, turning once. When cool enough to handle, place peeled garlic, tomatillos, jalapeño, onion, cilantro, and lime juice in food processor with salt. Pulse until ingredients are coarsely chopped, being careful not to over-process. Salsa should have substantial texture. Pour tomatillo mixture into bowl, and gently fold in mango pieces. The flavors will mingle and intensify if you let this sit at room temperature for an hour, covered, before serving.

This is terrific served with grilled fish and makes for an interesting change when served with chips as an appetizer.

Salsa Fresca (traditional salsa) – makes 3 cups

5 Roma tomatoes, coarsely chopped

1 teaspoon minced garlic

$\frac{1}{2}$ red onion, finely chopped

3 scallions, green parts only, finely sliced

$\frac{1}{4}$ cup fresh lime juice

2 jalapeños, cored and seeded, finely diced

4 tablespoons coarsely chopped fresh cilantro

$\frac{1}{2}$ tablespoon extra-virgin olive oil

$\frac{1}{2}$ tablespoon rice vinegar

salt and pepper to taste

Mix the first seven ingredients together well in a medium-size bowl. Add the olive oil, vinegar, salt, and pepper. Toss to blend. Let stand for 30 minutes at room temperature, then serve. If not served immediately, this may be refrigerated for up to 2 hours.

Bring back to room temperature before serving.

Salsa Rosa – serves 8

12 whole red bell peppers (about 4 cups when roasted and peeled)

½ cup plus 2 tablespoons extra-virgin olive oil, plus additional for coating peppers

1 tablespoon sea salt

2 whole Serrano chiles

6 garlic cloves

½ cup tomato purée

2 sprigs fresh oregano

¾ cup red wine vinegar

salt and pepper to taste

Preheat oven to 450°F. Coat peppers with olive oil, place on foil-lined baking sheet, and salt well. Bake in oven, turning every 10 minutes, until peppers are blistered and black, about 20–30 minutes. Remove from oven and place in brown paper bag or tightly covered glass bowl for 15–20 minutes. Peel and remove seeds, stems, and ribs. DO NOT RINSE, as this will diminish the flavor. Place in blender. Pour 2 tablespoons olive oil in hot sauté pan. Add the chiles and garlic. Then lower the heat to medium and cook, stirring occasionally, until the chiles are softened, blistered on all sides, and brown. Remove pan from heat, and let chiles and garlic cool in oil. Finely chop the garlic, add pinch of sea salt, and mash into paste. Add to the blender. Peel chiles and remove stems and seeds. Add to blender, along with tomato purée and oregano. Pour in remaining oil from sauté pan. Blend until smooth and thick. Turn a medium sauté pan with ¼ cup olive oil on high for 30 seconds. Slowly pour blender mixture into pan—STAND BACK, as it can splatter. Season with salt and pepper. Then whisk in remaining ¼ cup olive oil and the red wine vinegar. Ladle into canning jars and store in refrigerator for 1 week or freeze for up to 5 months.

To use with flank steak, season steak liberally with salt and pepper, then drizzle with olive oil. Grill the steak to medium rare on hot grill, about 4 minutes a side. Let rest 10 minutes. Then thinly slice the meat, cross-grain, and place on top of cooked spaghetti tossed with Salsa Rosa.

Tomato Relish – serves 10

3½ pounds heirloom or other meaty tomatoes (organic are best, so wait until you can pick some up at a farmers' market); use a variety for color

4 tablespoons minced shallots

3 garlic cloves, minced

2 tablespoons white balsamic vinegar

2 tablespoons chopped fresh chives

2 tablespoons Italian parsley

4 tablespoons extra-virgin olive oil

salt and pepper to taste

Coarsely chop the tomatoes, making every attempt to save the juices. Combine tomatoes and their juices in a medium bowl, and add the rest of the ingredients. Toss gently to mix well. Loosely cover bowl and let sit at room temperature until ready to serve.

Spoon a generous dollop over hot meat or fish and serve immediately.

Sauces

Berry Mint Sauce – makes 1¾ cups

2 cups chopped strawberries (about 1 pint)*
½ cup honey
¼ cup fresh mint leaves or fresh lemon verbena
2 tablespoons fresh lemon juice

Place strawberries, honey, and mint in small saucepan. Bring to a simmer and cook over medium heat for 1 minute or until honey dissolves. Place this mixture in food processor and blend until smooth. Strain to remove solids. Stir in lemon juice. Pour into container, cover, and refrigerate for up to 1 week.

May be served cold, at room temperature, or reheated. This is delicious over ice cream, cakes, and pancakes.

* Other berries may be used, but they will cook down more rapidly. If using blueberries, raspberries, blackberries, gooseberries, or others, you may want to increase the amount of berries by at least one half, that is, to 3 cups.

Strawberry Basil Compote – makes 1¼ cups

½ cup fresh orange juice

4 generous cups strawberries (about 30), stems removed and cut into quarters

20 large fresh basil leaves, coarsely chopped

1 teaspoon grated lemon zest

1 tablespoon honey

1 tablespoon balsamic vinegar

2 fresh mint leaves, chopped

In medium, non-metal saucepan, bring the orange juice, strawberries, basil, lemon zest, and honey to a boil over medium heat. Reduce heat to low and simmer until the juice is thick and syrupy, about 20 minutes. Stir in the vinegar, remove from heat, and cool to room temperature. Stir in chopped mint and serve.

Great over pound cake or ice cream or served as jam.

Rhubarb Compote – makes 3 cups

4 cups fresh or frozen rhubarb, cut into ½-inch pieces*

1 cup sugar

2 tablespoons fresh lemon juice

Combine ingredients in saucepan. Cook over medium heat, stirring until sugar is dissolved. Reduce heat to medium-low and simmer 10 minutes or until rhubarb is tender. Stir occasionally. Transfer to glass bowl, cover, and chill until cold.

 May be served cold, at room temperature, or warm. This is an excellent "sauce" to use over shortcake, pound cake, or angel food cake. Also delicious when served warm over waffles or with pancakes.

*Fresh rhubarb is much better, especially if you choose thin, reddish-pink stalks. FRESH always tastes better and certainly has a richer, more beautiful color!

Tequila-Lime Sauce – makes 2 cups

1¾ cups sugar

2 cups water

3 sprigs fresh garden mint

½ cup tequila (gold makes a richer flavor, but silver tequila works as well)

3 tablespoons fresh lime juice

Place sugar, water, and 2 sprigs of mint in a saucepan, and bring mixture to a boil. Reduce heat to simmer and cook for 20 minutes or until just beginning to thicken. Add the tequila and simmer 5 minutes more. Remove from heat and carefully stir in the lime juice. Let mixture cool. Strain through a medium-mesh colander to remove the mint. Discard the mint. May be refrigerated, tightly covered, for up to 2 days.

This is wonderful with fresh fruit or ice cream. It's even good served as a side with vanilla or plain yogurt as a breakfast item.

Tequila Lime Marinade – makes 2 cups

½ cup tequila (silver or gold)

1 cup fresh lime juice

½ cup fresh orange juice

zest from 1 fresh lime

zest from 1 fresh orange

1 tablespoon chile powder

2 garlic cloves, coarsely chopped

1 jalapeño, seeded and diced

1 teaspoon black pepper

2 teaspoons salt

Mix all ingredients together in large bowl. May be refrigerated, tightly covered, for up to 2 days.

This makes an excellent marinade for grilled flank or skirt steaks and grilled vegetables!

Chimichurri – makes 3 cups

1 packed cup fresh Italian parsley leaves

1 packed cup fresh cilantro leaves

½ cup packed fresh mint leaves

6 cloves garlic, coarsely chopped

1 teaspoon coarse salt

½ teaspoon ground pepper

1 teaspoon hot pepper flakes

⅓ cup cold water

⅓ cup distilled white or cider vinegar (or more, to taste)

1 cup extra-virgin olive oil

Combine the parsley, cilantro, mint, and garlic in a food processor and finely chop. Add the salt, pepper, and pepper flakes and process again to blend. Slowly add the water, vinegar, and olive oil to make a thick sauce.

This should be a highly seasoned sauce, so add salt and vinegar as necessary. If serving as a sauce, gently heat in saucepan right before needed. It works well with grilled beef, pork, lamb, and even chicken.

Spicy Citrus Sauce – makes 2 cups

1 cup molasses

½ cup fresh lime juice

3 teaspoons fresh lime zest

2 cups fresh orange juice

4 garlic cloves, coarsely chopped

8 chipotle chiles in adobo sauce (4-ounce can)

1 tablespoon extra-virgin olive oil

4 tablespoons unsalted butter, chilled and cut into 4 slices

Salt and pepper to taste

Using a food processor, purée molasses, lime juice and zest, orange juice, garlic, and chipotle chiles until smooth. Set aside. Just before serving, heat olive oil in shallow skillet over medium heat. Add molasses mixture. Simmer until thick and syrupy, about 2 minutes. Whisk in butter, one slice at a time. Season with salt and pepper.

Serve hot over grilled meat.

Red Chile Sauce – makes approximately 4 cups

  ¼ cup vegetable shortening

  5 teaspoons garlic, finely minced

  3 tablespoons flour

  1 16-ounce container frozen red chile, thawed

  2½ cups water

  2 teaspoons dried Mexican oregano

Melt shortening in heavy-duty pot over medium heat. Add minced garlic and stir until garlic is light brown. Slowly add flour and stir until you have a thick, brown paste. Do not burn. Then add red chile, water, and oregano and bring to a boil. Reduce heat and simmer for 30 minutes. Cover and simmer for additional 30 minutes. Let cool, then refrigerate, tightly covered. May be stored in refrigerator up to 2 weeks.

Guacamole – makes approximately 1 cup

  2 large, firm, ripe avocados

  ¼ cup grated onion

  1 cup tomato, seeded and finely chopped

  1 jalapeño, seeded and finely chopped

  2 garlic cloves, minced

  2 tablespoons fresh lemon juice

  salt and pepper to taste

With a large fork, mix all ingredients together in a glass or ceramic bowl. Mixture should be slightly chunky. Cover with plastic wrap, making sure that the plastic wrap covers the surface of the guacamole. This will keep it from turning brown. Refrigerate until ready to serve.

Green Chile Sauce –
makes approximately 4 cups

1 16-ounce package frozen green chile, thawed

1 small white onion, thinly sliced

2 garlic cloves, thinly sliced

2 tablespoons butter

1 14-ounce can fire-roasted, diced tomatoes or 6 Roma tomatoes, coarsely diced and roasted in 350° oven for 45 minutes

salt and additional butter to taste

Thaw green chile and pour into medium sauce pot. Then slice the onion and garlic cloves very thinly and sauté with butter, in small sauté pan over medium-low heat, for 30 minutes or until the onions begin to caramelize. Add the onion-garlic mixture and the tomatoes to the green chile and bring to a boil. Then immediately turn heat to medium-low and simmer for 1 hour. Remove from heat and let cool to room temperature. Then cover and refrigerate. Lasts up to 2 weeks in refrigerator.

Dressings

Champagne Vinaigrette– makes 2 cups

$\frac{1}{2}$ cup champagne vinegar

1 teaspoon sea salt

$1\frac{1}{2}$ cups extra-virgin olive oil

freshly ground black pepper to taste

Whisk the vinegar and salt together until the salt dissolves. Slowly whisk in the oil until the dressing is well blended. Season with pepper.

Dijon Vinaigrette – makes 1 cup

4 tablespoons Dijon mustard

8 tablespoons sherry vinegar

8 tablespoons fresh lemon juice

kosher salt to taste

freshly ground pepper

1 cup extra-virgin olive oil

Mix first five ingredients together well. Slowly whisk in olive oil and refrigerate until ready to use.

Lemon Dressing – makes 2 cups

½ cup lemon juice (2 large lemons), freshly squeezed

1 teaspoon salt

1¾ cups extra-virgin olive oil

freshly ground pepper

Whisk the lemon juice together with the salt until the salt dissolves. Slowly whisk in olive oil until well blended. Season with pepper to taste.

Sherry Shallot Vinaigrette – makes 1½ cups

¼ cup (4 large) shallots, finely diced

¾ teaspoon sea salt

⅓ cup sherry vinegar

1 cup extra-virgin olive oil

black pepper to taste

Whisk the shallots, salt, and vinegar together until the salt is dissolved. Slowly whisk in the oil until well blended. Season with pepper.

Creamy Dijon Dressing – makes 1 cup

½ cup mayonnaise

½ cup extra-virgin olive oil

6 tablespoons Dijon mustard

4 tablespoons champagne or white wine vinegar

salt and pepper

Whisk ingredients together in small bowl and season with salt and pepper. Cover, chill, and keep in refrigerator for up to 5 days.

Green Olive Dressing – makes 1 cup

⅔ cup extra-virgin olive oil

¼ cup seeded, chopped tomato

¼ cup finely chopped, pitted, brine-cured green olives
   (Sicilian are great!)

2 teaspoons lemon peel, grated

Mix all ingredients in small bowl. Season to taste with salt and pepper. Let stand at room temperature to blend flavors. Can be kept, tightly covered, in refrigerator for 5 days.

Bring to room temperature before using.

Orange-Fennel Vinaigrette – makes approximately ¾ cup

¼ cup fresh orange or blood orange juice

2 tablespoons minced shallots

1 tablespoon fresh thyme leaves

3 teaspoons grated orange peel

1 teaspoon honey

½ cup extra-virgin olive oil

¼ cup finely chopped fennel bulb

Mix first five ingredients together in small bowl. Slowly whisk olive oil into mixture until well blended. Add fennel bulb and stir gently. Can be refrigerated, covered, for up to 5 days.

Spring Herb Dressing – makes 1 cup

3 tablespoons finely chopped Italian parsley leaves

3 tablespoons finely chopped shallots

3 tablespoons fresh lemon juice

1 cup olive oil

½ cup champagne vinegar

2 teaspoons Dijon mustard

½ teaspoon salt

freshly ground pepper to taste

Combine all ingredients in small bowl and whisk briskly until well blended. Refrigerate until ready to use.

Bring to room temperature before serving.

Mustard Tarragon Vinaigrette – makes approximately ¾ cup

1 garlic clove, coarsely chopped

½ teaspoon sea salt

2 tablespoons fresh tarragon leaves, finely sliced and divided

2 teaspoons coarse mustard

2 small shallots, finely diced

2 tablespoons red wine vinegar

2 tablespoons sour cream

4 tablespoons extra-virgin olive oil

2 tablespoons fresh Italian parsley, finely chopped

2 teaspoons fresh chives or chervil, finely chopped

Pound the garlic in a mortar with the salt and 1 tablespoon of sliced tarragon until a smooth paste forms. Scrape into a 2-cup measuring cup. Slowly stir in the mustard until incorporated. Stir in the shallots and vinegar. Then gradually add the sour cream and olive oil, whisking until the sauce is smooth. Add the remaining tarragon, the parsley, and the chives. Season with more salt or vinegar if necessary. Let sit at room temperature until ready to serve, or you may cover and store in the refrigerator for up to 2 days.

Roquefort Vinaigrette – serves 10

4–6 ounces roquefort cheese

12 tablespoons extra-virgin olive oil

8 teaspoons sherry vinegar

4 tablespoons crème fraiche or sour cream

sea salt to taste

Combine the cheese, oil, and crème fraiche in a blender and blend until smooth. Scrape the mixture into a small bowl, and stir in the vinegar. Season to taste. Refrigerate until ready to use.

Herbed Lime Dressing – makes approximately 2½ cups

1 cup fresh lime juice

⅓ cup cider vinegar

1 garlic clove, pressed

3 teaspoons finely chopped fresh parsley

3 tablespoons finely chopped fresh tarragon

3 tablespoons finely chopped oregano

¾ teaspoon salt

¾ teaspoon freshly ground pepper

1 cup extra-virgin olive oil

Blend first eight ingredients together in small bowl. Slowly whisk in olive oil and continue to whisk until well blended. Store in refrigerator, tightly covered, for up to 5 days.

Bring back to room temperature when ready to use.

Simple Coleslaw Dressing – makes 1 cup

½ cup finely chopped parsley

½ cup extra-virgin olive oil

½ cup sherry vinegar

freshly ground pepper

salt

Whisk all ingredients together until well blended. Set aside until ready to use.

Desserts

Apricot Empanadas – makes 4 dozen small

Dough

2 cups unbleached flour

$\frac{1}{3}$ teaspoon sea salt

12 tablespoons (1$\frac{1}{2}$ sticks) unsalted butter, chilled and
  cut into small cubes

$\frac{1}{4}$ cup vegetable shortening, chilled

6 ounces cream cheese, room temperature

Apricot Filling

1$\frac{1}{4}$ cups dried apricots

1 cup fresh apricots

2 teaspoons cornstarch

2 tablespoons fruit brandy or 3 tablespoons triple sec

2 tablespoons sugar

$\frac{1}{2}$-inch piece of fresh ginger, peeled and pressed with
  a garlic press (use only the pulp that comes out of the
  bottom of the press—discard the fiber)

$\frac{1}{4}$ cup finely chopped piñons

$\frac{1}{4}$ cup dried bread crumbs

To prepare dough, combine the flour and salt in a food processor. Gradually add the butter, shortening, and cream cheese, pulsing briefly until the dough pulls away from the sides of the processor. Carefully remove dough from the processor and divide into 2 balls. Wrap each ball in plastic wrap and gently press into a disc. Refrigerate for at least 2 hours.

To prepare filling, coarsely chop dried apricots and let sit in bowl of hot water for 20 minutes. Pit the fresh apricots and cut into chunks. Then place in a saucepan and cook on medium until soft and mixture begins to resemble jam. Drain dried apricots and discard the liquid. Add cornstarch, dried apricots, liqueur, sugar, ginger, and piñons to sauce pan. Simmer until mixture begins to thicken, about 10 minutes more. Remove from heat and stir in the bread crumbs. Remove from heat and let cool to room temperature. This mixture will thicken even more as it cools.

Preheat oven to 375°F. Roll out each ball of dough to $\frac{1}{8}$-inch thickness. Using a 3–4" round cookie cutter, cut the dough into rounds. Top each round with 1 tablespoon of apricot filling. Fold the round in half, roll and pinch the edges together, then crimp to seal the edges with a damp fork. Continue this process until all the dough and filling has been used. Place the empanadas on a cookie sheet covered with parchment paper. Gently brush each one with an egg/water wash (1 egg well beaten with 1 tablespoon water) and sprinkle with sugar. Bake for 20 minutes or until empanadas are golden brown.

Santa Fe–Style Peach Pavlova – serves 10–12

9 egg whites

3 cups sugar

36 saltines, crushed

1½ cups chopped walnuts or pecans

3 teaspoons vanilla

3 teaspoons baking powder

pinch of salt

3 16-ounce packages frozen peaches, enough for a single layer of peaches

2 cups whipped cream

Preheat oven to 350°F. Beat egg whites in large mixing bowl until soft peaks form. Gradually fold in the sugar. Fold in saltines, nuts, vanilla, baking powder, and salt until well mixed. Pour into 10 x 12" baking dish and bake for 20–25 minutes or until brown and crusty. It will have the appearance of a large, flat meringue. Let cool completely. Lay peaches over baked mixture and cover with whipped cream.

Chill for several hours before serving.

Craig's St. Louis Gooey Butter Cake – serves 10–12

1 yellow cake mix

4 eggs

1 stick butter, melted

1 pound powdered sugar

8 ounces cream cheese

Preheat oven to 350°F. Blend cake mix with 2 eggs and butter. Spread into buttered 9 x 13" pan. Mix the remaining 2 eggs with the powdered sugar and cream cheese in a separate bowl. Whisk together until fluffy. Pour over top of cake mixture. Bake for 30 minutes or until golden brown.

Let completely cool before serving.

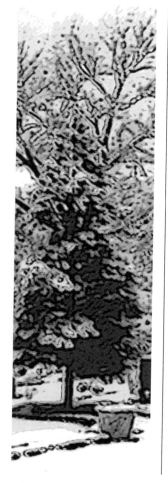

Coconut-Grilled Pineapple* – serves 8–10

2 ripe pineapples

8 ounces unsweetened coconut milk

3 cups turbinado (coarse brown) sugar or 3 cups white sugar

2 teaspoons cinnamon

2 teaspoons red chile powder (optional)

fresh mint sprigs, for garnish

Peel the pineapples. Slice into 1-inch slices. Then, using a melon baller or fruit corer, remove the fibrous core from the center of each slice. Discard the core. Shake the coconut milk well and pour into a shallow bowl. Pour the sugar into another shallow bowl; add the cinnamon and chile powder. Stir with a fork to mix well. Dip a pineapple slice into the coconut milk, then into the sugar mixture, shaking off the excess between dipping. Place on a wire rack with wax paper underneath (to minimize the mess). Continue process until all slices are coated. Preheat grill (charcoal or gas) to medium. Spray oil on the grill grate and place over the coals. Arrange the pineapple slices on the hot grill until nicely browned on both sides, about 4–6 minutes per side. Transfer pineapple to platter until ready to serve.

These can be served from the platter (garnish with fresh mint sprigs) as a simple dessert, or you can serve them in a bowl with homemade vanilla or coconut ice cream. They can be served either hot or cold.

*This recipe also works well with firm bananas, fresh nectarines, fresh peaches, or fresh apricots. Cut the bananas in half lengthwise, then again into quarters. Cut the other fruit in half, and remove the pits before dipping.

Jane's Toasted Sweet Cornbread*
with Berries – serves 10

Cornbread

* Can also be grilled on a charcoal or gas grill over medium heat. Place cornbread slices on greased grill rack and cook approximately 2 minutes or until slices are light brown on bottom. Carefully flip with large metal spatula and continue to grill until the other side is browned.

2 cups flour

2 cups yellow or white cornmeal

1/3 cup plus 4 teaspoons sugar

2 3/4 teaspoons ground cinnamon

1/4 teaspoon ground cumin

2 teaspoons baking powder

1 teaspoon salt

4 large eggs

2 cups buttermilk

10 tablespoons unsalted butter, melted and cooled

1/4 teaspoon red chile powder

Preheat oven to 375°F. Grease and flour two 9 x 5" glass loaf pans. Combine dry ingredients, using 1/3 cup of the sugar and 1 1/2 teaspoons of the ground cinamon, in large bowl and whisk to blend. In separate bowl, gently beat the eggs and mix in with buttermilk and butter, blending well. Pour liquid mixture over dry ingredients and stir, by hand, until just blended. Pour evenly into loaf pans and sprinkle with cinnamon-chile sugar (4 teaspoons sugar mixed with 1 1/4 teaspoons ground cinnamon and 1/4 teaspoon red chile powder). Bake 35–40 minutes or until the cornbread begins to pull away from sides of pan. Remove from oven and cool on wire rack. Unmold loaves and continue to cool to room temperature.

Using serrated knife, slice cornbread loaves into 1- to 1 1/2-inch slices. Place on baking sheet and broil for 4 minutes or until light brown. Remove from oven and place bread slices on wire cooling rack, broiled side down. Bring to room temperature.

Just before serving, place cooled bread pieces on baking sheet, broiled side down, and broil for 4 minutes or until second side is light brown.

Berry Topping

3½ pints fresh strawberries, sliced into quarters

3 pints fresh blackberries or blueberries

1 cup freshly squeezed orange juice or ¾ cup frozen orange
juice concentrate, thawed

4 tablespoons triple sec or 2 tablespoons fresh lime juice

1 teaspoon fruit-flavored brandy

2 tablespoons sugar

Place berries in small bowl. Mix remaining ingredients in
measuring cup and pour over berries. Let sit at room temperature
until ready to use.

After broiling or grilling the sweet cornbread, place the slices on
individual plates, and spoon berry topping generously over them.
Top with dollop of whipped cream and dash of remaining cinnamon-chile sugar.

Laura and Carol's SAR Apricot Bars – makes 9

Crust

1 cup flour

½ cup butter

¼ cup sugar

Preheat oven to 350°F. Lightly grease 9 x 9 x 2" baking dish. Combine flour, butter, and sugar in food processor until well blended. Press into prepared baking dish and bake 15 minutes. Remove from oven.

Filling

2 eggs

1 cup brown sugar

⅓ cup flour

¼ teaspoon salt

½ teaspoon baking powder

½ teaspoon vanilla

½ cup pecans, walnuts, almonds, or pinons, chopped

1–1½ cups apricots

½ cup date pieces (optional)

1 tablespoon orange juice (optional)

Process all the ingredients together in food processor. Pour over crust and bake 30 minutes. Let cool completely before cutting.

Pie Crust – makes four 9-inch crusts

4 cups flour

2 teaspoons sugar

1 teaspoon sea salt

1¾ cups plus 2 tablespoons solid vegetable shortening

1 large egg

2 tablespoons champagne vinegar
(cider vinegar works just as well)

1 tablespoons water

Place the flour, sugar, and salt in a large bowl. Add shortening and mix with a fork until the mixture is crumbly. In a separate bowl, mix the egg, vinegar, and water. Add the egg mixture to the flour mixture, combining until the flour is moist and the mixture holds together. Then divide the dough into 4 equal portions, shaping each one into a flattened disk. Wrap each disk tightly in plastic and refrigerate at least 30 minutes before using.

The dough can be refrigerated up to 1 week or frozen up to 1 month. Defrost the crust overnight in the refrigerator before use.

The Banana in the Brandy Bottle

The midweek night was pitch black and full of swirling flakes that raised the snowfall level to well over a foot. The seminar participants had just been dropped off at the Seminar House after our one night-on-the-town, where we had dined together sumptuously. Suddenly—poof!—the power failed and the lights went out!

We all stood dumbstruck—or maybe savoring the unusual moment of total darkness and quiet. Someone clicked on a lighter and strode into the kitchen to find some candles. Not long after, a flickering calm settled over the Seminar Room as everyone found a seat to figure out what to do next. The night was still young, not yet nine o'clock. For a time, no one spoke.

Then Dick Gould* piped up cheerily, "Would anyone like to see the banana in a brandy bottle trick?" With no reading lights or planned agenda, it seemed like a good idea at the time because one knew what the banana in a brandy bottle trick was and archaeologists are curious by nature.

---

* Richard Gould edited *Explorations in Ethnoarchaeology* and *Shipwreck Anthropology* for the School for Advanced Research, in addition to authoring many other books.

With intrepid Gould in the lead, an expedition party entered the kitchen and soon discovered a cache of liquor. "First, we need an empty bottle," said Gould. In the blink of an eye, an already open brandy bottle was pulled off the shelf, and glasses were filled all 'round. "Just leave a dribble in the bottom of the bottle," cautioned Gould. "And find me a banana."

As some savored the brandy, others searched until they discovered several bananas—a bunch of five, as I recollect.

Back comfortably in our seats, we watched Gould place the brandy bottle, with just a swirl still left inside, on a small table in the center of the seminar room. Next to the bottle, he placed a book of matches he had taken from the kitchen. Then he pulled the peel of one banana about 2 inches down, exposing the top of the ripe fruit.

"Watch carefully," said Gould as he swirled the brandy around the bottle, placed it back on the table, and lit a match. He stood there quietly for a moment with the lighted match in one hand and the partly peeled banana in the other. The rapt audience looked from the long narrow neck of the brandy bottle to the banana—which was about twice the diameter of the bottle's neck—and then back to the bottle. Mouths gaped, but no words came out.

With what seemed to be one smooth movement, Gould dropped

the match into the bottle's narrow neck and placed the tip of the banana flush against the neck's lip.

An instant of utter silence was followed by an appalling mixture of sucking and squishing sounds and then a loud, echoing thud as if something heavy had been dropped into an empty well.

As we all rushed up to take a closer look, Gould smiled and held up a vacated banana peel. Sure enough, there, curled on the glass bottom inside the narrow-necked brandy bottle, was a whole fat banana.

Amidst many congratulations to Gould, someone suggested, "Let's do it again." No one objected, so another bottle was pulled down from the shelf…

Early the next morning when our faithful cooks arrived, they found many glasses of brandy, some totally full, as if they were used not as drinking vessels but only as containers. They also discovered in the center of the seminar room a small table bearing five brandy bottles, empty except for a single naked banana in each.

I can only imagine what stories the cooks conjured up to tell their friends and family about the exotic rituals of archaeologists.… Ah, but few were probably stranger than the truth.

—W. L. Rathje, member of the 1978 "Explorations in Ethnoarchaeology" seminar and author of *Rubbish!: The Archaeology of Garbage*

Index